AF606910

SIMP SONI STAS

VOL. 7

Tales from New Literary Project

SIMPSONISTAS

VOL. 7

EDITED BY JOSEPH DI PRISCO

RARE BIRD
LOS ANGELES, CALIF.

THIS IS A GENUINE RARE BIRD BOOK

Rare Bird Books
6044 North Figueroa Street
Los Angeles, California 90042
rarebirdbooks.com

Copyright © 2025 by Joseph Di Prisco

FIRST TRADE PAPERBACK ORIGINAL EDITION

All rights reserved, including the right to reproduce this book or portions thereof in any form whatsoever, including but not limited to print, audio, and electronic.

For more information, address:
Rare Bird Books Subsidiary Rights Department
6044 North Figueroa Street
Los Angeles, California 90042

This is a work of fiction and a product of the author's imagination. Names, characters, businesses, places, events, and incidents are used in a fictitious manner. Any resemblance to actual persons, living or dead, or actual events is purely coincidental.

Set in Minion
Printed in the United States

Proceeds from book sales go toward supporting the work of the nonprofit New Literary Project, newliteraryproject.org

10 9 8 7 6 5 4 3 2 1

Library of Congress Cataloging-in-Publication Data available upon request

Dedicated in memoriam to
Donald A. McQuade
Teacher, Writer, Scholar, Editor, Leader, Visionary

New Literary Project Tenth Anniversary
Mixing It Up Since 2015

CONTENTS

People, Places, & Things: A Miscellany *11*
Preface: "How I Founded a Nonprofit—Even If I'm Not Always Sure I Did: 20 (and Counting) Easy Lessons I Keep Learning": Joseph Di Prisco *23*

PART ONE

2025 Joyce Carol Oates Prizes *33*
Say Hello to My Little Friend, an excerpt from the novel, Jennine Capó Crucet *37*
The Horse, an excerpt from the novel, Willy Vlautin *51*
Don't Skip Out on Me, an excerpt from the novel, Willy Vlautin *56*
"Why Is Your Writing So Violent?": an essay by Joyce Carol Oates *62*
"The American Dream": A Course Syllabus, by Joyce Carol Oates *66*
"The Plunge," a story, JR Murray *74*
Three Poems, Ralph J. Long Jr. *85*
"What About Writers?!," an essay, Michael Ross *87*
"The Palace," a poem, Heather Tone *91*
"Whirling," a story, H. L. Onstad *93*
"Call and Response," an essay, Laura Cogan *103*
"Laidlaw," a story, Chris Feliciano Arnold *112*

PART TWO

NEWLIT CREATIVE WRITING WORKSHOPS;
WRITING FROM STUDENTS, INSTRUCTORS, AND ALUMNI

Albany High School; Concord High School; East Bay Center for the Performing Arts; Emery High School; Girls Inc of Alameda County; Leadership Public Schools Hayward (LPS); Mt. McKinley High School, Contra Costa County Juvenile Hall (2022–2024); Northgate High School.

"Did You Hear Her Drowning?": Zara Sharza *131*
"Dos barras de chocolate, el anhelo de un corazón," Anali Pascual *133*
Two Poems, Violet Ferreira *135*
Poem, Alexis Montifar *137*
"Balance Beam," Yarelie *138*
"The Darkness of a Man's World": A collaborative poem; K. Emanuelle Mendoza, Eifa Lam-Triplett, Enaya Buksh, Sophia Ruiz-Braz *139*
"Musica Mon Amour," Lina Ihaddadene *141*
"Our Walk to the Train," Erica Matias *144*
"Within Us," Kalaijah Walker *145*
[Untitled], Katharine Kho 147

"On the Question of race," Ingrid Molina Arellano *149*
"Growing Into Me," Lyrick Harris *152*
"Dance," Kalia Griffin *153*
Writing from Mt. McKinley High School,
Contra Costa County Juvenile Hall 2022–2024 *155*
Three Poems, David Wood *162*
"Keep on Keeping On," a story, Rayjon Briscoe Young *164*
"When I Heard the News Roe v Wade was Struck Down," a poem, Isa Maloof *173*
"Red, White, & Blue," an essay by Genay Markham *174*
Two Poems, Grace Decker *179*
"Who Needs Poetry.": an essay, Drew Kiser *182*

PART THREE

"Demolition," a story, Fiona McFarlane *189*
Four Poems, William Archila *204*
Five Poems, Matthew Zapruder *208*
"Are You Happy?" a story, Lori Ostlund *220*

Contributors *236*

ACKNOWLEDGMENTS & PERMISSIONS

Grateful thanks for generous counsel and assistance, editorial, and otherwise, to:

Diane Del Signore
Amy Baker
Hannah Bishop
Laura Cogan
Tyson Cornell
Abigail Donahue
Victoria Fox
Joyce Carol Oates
Tim O'Connell
Hannah Onstad

"The American Dream": A Course Syllabus, by Joyce Carol Oates.
"Exploring the meaning of The American Dream through American literature and film."
Reprinted from *Joyce Carol Oates: A Writer's Journal Substack*,
with permission from the author.

"Are You Happy?," a story excerpted from *Are You Happy?* by Lori Ostlund.
Copyright © 2025 by Lori Ostlund. Published on May 6, 2025, by Astra Publishing House.
Reprinted by permission.

"Demolition," from *Highway Thirteen* by Fiona McFarlane.
Copyright © 2024 by Fiona McFarlane.
Reprinted by permission of Farrar, Straus and Giroux. All Rights Reserved.

An excerpt from *Don't Skip Out on Me*, a novel by Willy Vlautin.
Copyright © 2018 by Willy Vlautin. Published by HarperCollins Publishers.
Reprinted with permission.

An excerpt from *The Horse*, a novel by Willy Vlautin.
Copyright © 2024 by Willy Vlautin. Published by HarperCollins Publishers.
Reprinted with permission.

"Laidlaw," by Chris Feliciano Arnold, originally published in *Ecotone*.

"The Plunge," by JR Murray, originally published in *The Opiate.*

Poems by William Archila, reprinted from *S is For,* Black Lawrence Press.

Poems by Ralph J. Long Jr.: "Dermatology" first appeared in the *Anacapa Review*, 2025.

"Enough" appeared on the web in Maya's Micros
—a presentation of The Closed Eye Open, 2024.

"Thinking About Home on the 4th of July" appeared in Peregrine, 2022.

Poems by Matthew Zapruder:
"For Young Poets," "La Plague," "Thus"
appeared in *I Love Hearing Your Dreams.*
Copyright © 2024 by Matthew Zapruder. Published by Scribner.

"Dirty Tesla" originally appeared in *Divagations.*

"Say Hello to My Little Friend,"
an excerpt from *Say Hello to My Little Friend* by Jennine Capó Crucet.
Copyright 2024 © by Jennine Capó Crucet.
Reprinted by permission of Simon & Schuster, an Imprint of Simon & Schuster, LLC.

"Whirling," by H. L. Onstad, first published in *Solstice Literary Magazine.*

"Why Is Your Writing So Violent?" by Joyce Carol Oates.
Reprinted from *Joyce Carol Oates: A Writer's Journal Substack*,
with permission from the author.
Originally published in *The New York Times*, March 29, 1981.

Original, previously unpublished work printed with permission of the authors.

Simpsonistas: Tales from the Simpson Literary Project Vol. 1 (2018)
Simpsonistas: Tales from the Simpson Literary Project Vol. 2 (2019)
Simpsonistas: Tales from the Simpson Literary Project Vol. 3 (2021)
Simpsonistas: Tales from New Literary Project Vol. 4 (2022)
Simpsonistas: Tales from New Literary Project Vol. 5 (2023)
Simpsonistas: Tales from New Literary Project Vol. 6 (2024)
Simponistas: Tales from New Literary Project Vol. 7 (2025)

Series Editor: Joseph Di Prisco

PEOPLE, PLACES, & THINGS
A MISCELLANY: 2025
NEW LITERARY PROJECT: FOUNDED 2015

The University of California, Berkeley, English Department

Department Chairs, 2015–2025:
Prof. Genaro Padilla, Prof. Steven Justice, Prof. Ian Duncan, Prof. Eric Falci
Prof. Elisa Tamarkin.
NewLit Workshop Directors, 2017–2025:
Prof. Scott Saul; Prof. Geoffrey O'Brien; Prof. Fiona McFarlane; Prof. Cecil Giscombe.

Bonnie Bonetti-Bell Writing Workshops, Spring 2025:

Albany High School, Albany, California: Molly Montgomery, faculty.
Contra Costa County Juvenile Hall, Martinez, California; Mt. McKinley School, Contra Costa County Office of Education. Brian Murtagh, Principal.
Girls Inc. of Alameda County, Oakland, California: Julayne Virgil, CEO; Virgtrese McGee, Gabi Reyes-Acosta, Jazmin Noble, Aja Holland, Carina Silva.
Northgate High School, Walnut Creek, California: Mount Diablo Unified School District; David Wood and Aliza Selinger, faculty.

Saint Mary's College of California , MFA Creative Writing Program

Prof. Chris Feliciano Arnold, Director, and Chair of Creative Writing Programs

Iris Starn Writing Workshops, Spring 2025:
Concord High School, Concord, California: Gabrielle Loitz, faculty.
East Bay Center for the Performing Arts, Richmond, California: Kwesi Anku, faculty.
Emery High School, Emeryville, California: Mignon Combs, faculty.
Leadership Public Schools—Hayward, Hayward, California:
Huey Collette and Adam White, faculty.

Bonnie Bonetti-Bell Fellows & Workshops

(once upon a time Simpson Fellows & Workshops)
2017–2025

Workshops led by Cal graduate student creative writing instructors, offered free of charge to 700+ students over nine years and continuing.
University of California, Berkeley, English Department

Prof. Cecil Giscombe, Director

2025

Albany High School
Laura Ritland

Girls Inc. of Alameda County
Edil Hassan
Camille Santana Considine

Mt. McKinley School at Contra Costa County Juvenile Hall
Drew V. Kiser

Northgate High School
Ryan Lackey

Fellows: 2017–2025
Ariel Baker-Gibbs
Uttara Chintamani Chaudhuri
Frank Cruz
Katherine Ding
Delarys Ramos Estrada
Mehak Faisal Khan
Lise Gaston
Edil Hassan
John James
Naima Karczmar
Andrew David King
Drew V. Kiser
Ryan Lackey
Jessica Laser
Eric Moscosky
Ismail Muhammad
Laura Ritland
Camille Santana Considine
Alex Ullman
Noah Warren
Rosetta Young

Iris Starn Fellows & Workshop Leaders, 2023–2024

Workshops led by Saint Mary's creative writing instructors, offered free of charge to 300+ students over three years, and continuing.
Saint Mary's College of California, MFA Creative Writing Program.

Prof. Chris Feliciano Arnold, MFA Director

2025

Concord High School
Courtney Pazin

East Bay Center for the Performing Arts
Genay Markham

Emery High School:
Rayjon Briscoe Young

Leadership Public Schools—Hayward
Isa Maloof

Fellows: 2023–2025
Camila Elizabet Aguirre Aguilar
Carly Blackwell
Rayjon Briscoe Young
Isa Maloof
Genay Markham
Courtney Pazin
Allie Silvas

Jack Hazard Fellows, 2022–2025

Creative Writers Teaching High School
Summer Writing Fellowship of $5,000

Thirty-eight writers from schools in fifteen states have been awarded Jack Hazards

Prof. Ian Maloney, Director

2025 Jack Hazard Fellows & Writing Projects

Kristin Collier
St. Paul Academy and Summit School (St. Paul, Minnesota)
What Debt Demands

Dallas Crow
Woodward Academy (College Park, Georgia)
Satie in Wyoming

Will Ejzak
Gwendolyn Brooks College Prep Academy (Chicago, Illinois)
The Witch

Molly Olguín
The Bush School (Seattle, Washington)
The Girl is Going to Live

Anjoli Roy
Punahou School (Honolulu, Hawaii)
Fatherland

2024 Jack Hazard Fellows & Writing Projects:

Cyd A. Apellido
The Fletcher School (Charlotte, North Carolina)
Beneath Her Shadow (a novel)

Sean Gleason
Rudsdale High School (Oakland, California)
On The Bricks

Mohammad Hakima
The International High School for Health Sciences (Queens, New York)
A Leak in the Roof (memoir/essays)

Monica Judge
Bethesda-Chevy Chase High School (Bethesda, Maryland)
Elemental (an essay collection)

Chad Marsh
Lake Washington High School (Kirkland, Washington)
The Lighter Graveyard; Fairfield (a novel)

Natalie Mislang Mann
Vaughn International Studies Academy, VISA High School (Pacoima, California)
Roots of a Banyan Tree (a memoir)

Sarah Schiff
The Paideia School (Atlanta, Georgia)
This Accidental World (a novel)

Heather Tone
St. Andrew's Episcopal Upper School (Austin, Texas)
This Moment Moves Us Forward

Alonzo Vereen
Sidwell Friends School (Washington, DC)
The Mean Girls of Morehouse (a novel)

Adam White
St. Sebastian's School (Needham, Massachusetts)
The Island Rule (a novel)

2023 Jack Hazard Fellows

William Archila
STEAM Virtual Academy (Los Angeles, California)

Victoria María Castells
Miami Arts Charter School (Miami, Florida)

Leticia Del Toro
Campolindo High School (Moraga, California)

Elizabeth DiNuzzo
The Albany Academies (Albany, New York)

t'ai freedom ford
Benjamin Banneker Academy (Brooklyn, New York)

Emily Y. Harnett
The Haverford School (Haverford, Pennsylvania)

Jeff Kass
Pioneer High School (Ann Arbor, Michigan)

Ariana D. Kelly
Boston University Academy (Boston, Massachusetts)

Kate McQuade
Phillips Academy (Andover, Massachusetts)

Tyson Morgan
Crystal Springs Uplands School (Hillsborough, California)

Shareen K. Murayama
Henry J. Kaiser High School (Honolulu, Hawaii)

Sahar Mustafah
Homewood-Flossmoor High School (Flossmoor, Illinois)

Ky-Phong Tran
Long Beach Renaissance High School for the Arts (Long Beach, California)

Vernon Clifford Wilson
Horace Mann School (Bronx, New York)

2022 Jack Hazard Fellows (California)

Kevin Allardice
Albany High School (Albany, California)
Julie T. Anderson
The College Preparatory School (Oakland, California)
Armando Batista
Pacific Ridge School (Carlsbad, California)
Adam O. Davis
The Bishop's School (La Jolla, California)
Sheila Madary
Saint Mary's High School (Stockton, California)
Molly Montgomery
Emery High School (Emeryville, California)
Mehnaz Sahibzada
New Roads School (Santa Monica, California)
Tori Sciacca
Richmond High School (Richmond, California)
Andy Spear
Head-Royce School (Oakland, California)

Joyce Carol Oates Prize 2017–2025

Awarded annually, a prize of $50,000, not for a book, but to a distinguished mid-career author of fiction, that is, one who has emerged and is still emerging; given in testament of consequential literary achievement as well as in support of work to come.

2025 Finalists and Recipients with then-current works of fiction

Jennine Capó Crucet, North Carolina, *Say Hello to My Little Friend* (Simon & Schuster) Prize Recipient
Sarah Manguso, California, *Liars* (Hogarth)
Julia Phillips, New York, *Bear* (Hogarth)
Morgan Talty, Maine, *Fire Exit* (Tin House)
Willy Vlautin, Oregon, *The Horse* (HarperCollins) Prize Recipient

2025 JCO Prize Longlisted Authors & Most Recent Book of Fiction

Rumaan Alam, *Entitlement*, Riverhead
Jami Attenberg, *A Reason to See You Again*, Ecco
Marie-Helene Bertino, *Beautyland*, FSG
Venita Blackburn, *Dead in Long Beach, California*, MCD
Rita Bullwinkel, *Headshot*, Viking
Ryan Chapman, *The Audacity*, Soho
Jennine Capó Crucet, *Say Hello to My Little Friend*, Simon & Schuster
Leif Enger, *I Cheerfully Refuse*, Grove Atlantic
Amina Gautier, *The Best That You Can Do*, Soft Skull
Thomas Grattan, *In Tongues*, MCD
Abby Geni, *The Body Farm*, Counterpoint
Cristina Henríquez, *The Great Divide*, Ecco
Maria Hummel, *Goldenseal*, Counterpoint
Miranda July, *All Fours*, Riverhead
Porochista Khakpour, *Tehrangeles*, Pantheon
Crystal Hana Kim, *The Stone Home*, William Morrow / HarperCollins
Lisa Ko, *Memory Piece*, Riverhead
R. O. Kwon, *Exhibit*, Riverhead
Caroline Leavitt, *Days of Wonder*, Algonquin
Hilary Leichter, *Terrace Story*, Ecco
Sarah Manguso, *Liars*, Hogarth
Chigozie Obioma, *The Road to the Country*, Hogarth
Tommy Orange, *Wandering Stars*, Knopf
Kimberly King Parsons, *We Were the Universe*, Knopf
Julia Phillips, *Bear*, Hogarth
Andrew Porter, *The Disappeared*, Knopf
Regina Porter, *The Rich People Have Gone Away*, Hogarth
Rudy Ruiz, *The Border Between Us*, Blackstone

Danzy Senna, *Colored Television*, Riverhead
Morgan Talty, *Fire Exit*, Tin House
Laura van den Berg, *State of Paradise*, FSG
Willy Vlautin, *The Horse*, Harper

2024 Finalists and Recipient

Jamel Brinkley
Patricia Engel
Ben Fountain (Prize Recipient)
Idra Novey
Bennett Sims

2023 Finalists and Recipient

Rabih Alameddine
Clare Beams
James Hannaham
David Means
Manuel Muñoz (Prize Recipient)

2022 Finalists and Recipient

Christopher Beha
Percival Everett
Lauren Groff (Prize Recipient)
Katie Kitamura
Jason Mott

2021 Finalists and Recipient

Danielle Evans (Prize Recipient)
Jenny Offill
Darin Strauss
Lysley Tenorio

2020 Finalists and Recipient

Chris Bachelder
Maria Dahvana Headley
Rebecca Makkai
Daniel Mason (Prize Recipient)
Peter Orner
Dexter Palmer
Kevin Wilson

2019 Finalists and Recipient

Rachel Kushner
Laila Lalami (Prize Recipient)
Valeria Luiselli
Sigrid Nunez
Anne Raeff
Amor Towles

2018 Finalists and Recipient

Ben Fountain
Samantha Hunt
Karan Mahajan
Anthony Marra (Prize Recipient)
Martin Pousson

2017 Finalists and Recipient

T. Geronimo Johnson (Prize Recipient)
Valeria Luiselli
Lori Ostlund
Dana Spiotta

Joyce Carol Oates Prize Longlist and Finalist Publishers: 2017–2025

333 Longlisted Authors (56 publishers)
41 Shortlisted Finalists (26 publishers)
10 Prize Winners (8 publishers)

Longlist publishers with number of their authors considered

Algonquin (11)
Avid Reader (1)
Back Bay (1)
Ballantine (2)
Bellevue Literary (4)
Blackstone (1)
Bloomsbury (6)
Catapult (4)
Celadon (1)
Coffee House (1) 1 finalist
Counterpoint (15) 1 finalist
Crooked Media Reads (1)
Custom House (1)
Delphinium (2)
Dial (2)
Doubleday (7) 1 finalist
Dutton (4) 1 finalist

Dzanc (1)
Ecco (24) 3 finalists
Elixir (1)
Flatiron (3) (**2024 Prize Recipient**) 1 finalist
FSG (17) four finalists
Grand Central (1)
Graywolf (9) (**2023 Prize Recipient**) 2 finalists
Grove Atlantic (9) 1 finalist
Harper Collins (5) (**2017 Prize Recipient) (2025 Prize Recipient**) 2 finalists
Henry Holt (1)
Hogarth (8) (**2018 Prize Recipient**) 3 finalists
HoughtonMiflin (4)
Knopf (14) 2 finalists
Little Brown (17) (**2020 Prize Recipient**) 3 finalists
Mariner (2)
MCD (9) 1 finalist
Melville House (1)
Nan A. Talese (1)
New York Review of Books (1)
Norton (9) 1 finalist
One World (1)
Pantheon (3) (**2019 Prize Recipient**) 2 finalists
Penguin (16) 1 finalist
Picador (2)
Putnam (6)
Random House (10) 1 finalist
Rare Bird (3) 1 finalist
Riverhead (34) (**2021 and 2022 Prize Recipients**) 4 finalists
Scribner (3) 3 finalists
Simon Schuster (8) (**2025 Prize Recipient**) 1 finalist
Soft Skull (2)
Soho (7)
St. Martin (4)
Tim Duggan (1)
Tin House (5) 2 finalists
Triquarterly Books (1)
Two Dollar Radio (1) 1 finalist
Viking (8) 3 finalists
Zibby Books (1)

Jurors of the Joyce Carol Oates Prize 2017–2024

Heidi Benson
Anne Cain
Laura Cogan
Professor Mark Danner, Berkeley
Joseph Di Prisco
Professor Joshua Gang, Berkeley
Jane Hu
Professor Donna Jones, Berkeley
Regan McMahon
Professor Ian Maloney, St. Francis College, Brooklyn
Professor Geoffrey O'Brien, Berkeley
Professor Katherine Snyder, Berkeley
Professor Hertha Dawn Sweet Wong, Berkeley
David Wood
Professor Dora Zhang, Berkeley

Judges for the Joyce Carol Oates Prize:

New Literary Project Board of Directors judges and determines recipients of the Prize

Board of Directors

Joseph Di Prisco
Chair, Author & Educator
Diane Del Signore
Executive Director
Shanti Ariker
Chief Legal Officer, JFrog
James Bell
Founder & Chairman, Bell Investment Advisors; Community Leader
Uttara Chintamani Chaudhuri
PhD Candidate, UC Berkeley English. Bonnie Bonetti-Bell Fellow.
Creative Writing Teacher.
Laura Cogan
Editor and Consultant
Ian Duncan
English Department Chair Emeritus, UC Berkeley;
Florence Green Bixby Professor of English
Ben Fountain
Author, Educator
Manuel Muñoz
Author, Professor, University of Arizona
John Murray
Author and Associate Professor (Teaching) (retired), University of Southern California

Joyce Carol Oates (Honorary Director)
Author and Professor of Humanities, Princeton University
Pat Scott
Public Radio and Nonprofit Executive
Frank Starn
Community Leader and Corporate Executive
Elisa Tamarkin
English Department Chair & Professor, University of California, Berkeley
Katharine Bixby Hotchkis Chair in English
David Wood
Community Leader and Public High School English Teacher

Director Emeritus/Emerita

Eric Falci
English Department Chair, University of California, Berkeley
Donald McQuade
English Professor Emeritus; Vice Chancellor Emeritus, University of California, Berkeley
Beth Needel
Executive Director, Lafayette Library and Learning Center Foundation
Genaro Padilla
Chair and Professor Emeritus, English Department; Vice Chancellor Emeritus; University of California, Berkeley
Michael Ross
Author, US & International Law School & University Lecturer

NewLit Team

Diane Del Signore, Executive Director
Camila Aguirre Aguilar, Project Developer & Coordinator
Abigail Donahue, Project Manager
Hannah Onstad, Communication Director
Kristina Sepetys, Chief Evangelist
Tyson Cornell, Rare Bird, Publisher
Josephine Courant, Digital Design

New Literary Project Supporters

Abundant, humble gratitude for all our generous donors who have sustained the work of the not-for-profit New Literary Project since our founding in 2015: newliteraryproject.org

"Write your heart out."
—Joyce Carol Oates

PREFACE

HOW I FOUNDED A NONPROFIT—
THOUGH I'M NOT ALWAYS SURE I DID:
20 (AND COUNTING) EASY LESSONS I KEEP LEARNING

June 10, 2025

"What's it like starting a nonprofit?" My good friend wanted to know.

"I learn something every day," I said.

And he said, "That bad, huh?"

Even so, New Literary Project has been mixing it up since 2015. That means NewLit, a 501(c)(3) nonprofit, is celebrating our tenth anniversary with our own extraordinary roadshow—readings, celebrations, workshops, and the release of *Simpsonistas: Tales from New Literary Project. Vol. 7.*

From the jump, did I appreciate what I was getting into? Yes and no. For twenty-some years, I'd served on enterprising nonprofit boards dedicated to the arts, education, children's health, and theater, and chaired a board of directors of a remarkable school in Oakland for seven years, but creating something out of whole cloth would turn out to be categorically different.

I'm called the founder of NewLit, and it's not exactly wrong, but lately I've been rethinking what that means. Along the way, it turns out, I really did learn, and re-learn, something every day.

Lesson 1

Should never have done it. It was too hard. Life is too short. I would be dismayed in ways I never saw coming.

Lesson 2

Best thing I ever did. Life is too short not to have done it. I was exhilarated in ways I never expected. Mostly, I learned the obvious, that I could never do this by myself. Some days I hardly mattered. Those were uplifting days.

Lesson 3

I knew NewLit had a distinct mission and vision and purpose. Which reminds me: we found ourselves wordsmithing mission statements till we wanted to cry. Crying has an honored place in nonprofits, if not in baseball. (What a conundrum: to know the mission and you still search for words to express it.)

Lesson 4

This became our message, distilled over time: "The choice is clear. Fund the arts. As much as you can. Educate kids, support artists. Yes, the planet needs rescuing, and people need food and housing and health care. The world needs all that and more. The world also needs the nourishment, refuge, and attention of the arts. Young people who are marginalized—now speaking in their own voices. Writers now telling, and teachers now teaching, the stories of our lives. That's what helps make democracy a democracy. That's what NewLit is doing. Thank you for choosing to join with us." (Not exactly an elevator pitch. Which is fine by us. Because sometimes it's healthier to take the stairs.)

Lesson 5

Over the course of these often tumultuous ten years, this is what we have accomplished: We have awarded ten Joyce Carol Oates Prizes for outstanding mid-career fiction authors. Funded thirty-eight Jack Hazard Fellows, remarkable writers who teach high school in fourteen states. Taught over a thousand teenagers in twenty-eight workshops offered at no cost throughout the Bay Area. Sustained teaching fellowships for twenty-eight graduate student writers from UC Berkeley and Saint Mary's College who lead the workshops. Curated seven volumes of *Simpsonistas: Tales from New Literary Project, Vol. 7* of which is now in your hands and nationally distributed, featuring distinguished authors such as Joyce Carol Oates and JCO Prize Winners published alongside two-hundred forty younger writers from our workshops. Let's hurry to the next lesson.

Lesson 6

Next time we should avoid building a nonprofit during a worldwide pandemic. Or during the chaotic administration of a president bent on eviscerating arts and sciences. At NewLit, however, we couldn't avoid either condition. In early March 2020, we approved our first strategic plan, mere days before the world's wheels officially fell off. If you recall those mask-no-mask, hose-down-the-mail, toilet-paper-shortage, vaccine-to-come days, you might appreciate that nobody has ever consulted that stratplan since. Not to worry. We recently approved our updated strategic plan, titled "Stay a Start-up Forever." That made pretty good sense, too.

Lesson 7

I learned how we could enlist good-hearted, brick-solid, wildly imaginative, hard-working colleagues and donors to keep us company, and learn from them, especially when they were right and even when I thought they might not be, because it's all about engagement, investment, commitment. (That's why we never send out an email that goes, "Dear All." Who talks like that and why should anybody open that message?) It was beyond fortunate for us that from the outset we had tremendous partners: the University of California, Berkeley, English Department and more recently the MFA Department at Saint Mary's College of California. Moral of the story: find your people, earn colleagues, make your big tent bigger all the time.

Lesson 8

It's a tic of mine, but I cringe over stock terms like "charity" and "charitable contribution." The patronizing connotations grate in my ear. To be clear, I am not insane: I am all for tax deductions; consult with your financial advisor, we are not providing legal counsel. As for legal counsel, have on your board—oh, wait, you really need a wise and strategic and generous board, an encompassing topic unto itself. We needed to have on our board at least two great lawyers. Since every lawyer presumes they are the dispositive authority on everything (which I say with grudging respect), we recruited another lawyer for balance.

Lesson 9

Oh, man, the bureaucracy, the infrastructure. We fortunately brought into the fold in year four our charismatic executive director, someone with the most prestigious MBA, Stanford Business School. She was our first employee and is somebody who reads more than I do and also thinks strategically. And infrastructure accounts for less than half her job, all the while leading a strong, big-hearted NewLit team. We needed somebody just like her (whoever you are, don't even think about poaching) to deal with things like: Articles of Incorporation. Payroll. Banking. Consultants. Federal and state oversight. And so on and so on, including the infamous 990s. (I had so much to learn about 990s; I packed a lunch.)

Lesson 10

This one is embarrassing. I was contemplating mission and programs 24/7. Call me naïve, but I sometimes found it hard to understand how anybody could legitimately be, well, doing anything else. While I was contemplating fundraising, strategy, planning, organizing, other people were going about—I guess the concept would be—living their lives. To succeed, we needed to bring to life exactly how our nonprofit intersected with their values. Because…

Lesson 11

That's moneyball right there. And that intersection happened when we gave people something that meant in and to and for their lives. When we gave them something to talk about. Gave them something worth giving to. Gave them a reason to read our newsletter (and made it a nourishing and stylish regular newsletter that we hoped nobody unsubscribed from and had fun with it). We threw good parties. Really good parties. With a very hot DJ. We didn't do galas with paddle-raises: who likes paddle-raises and the gala concept? This relationship with donors had nothing to do with swag like tote bags. (Just asking: How many lonely tote bags are unceremoniously cast off into the darker regions of car trunks?)

Lesson 12

We never forgot what the Godfather said: Keep your friends close. (He added something about keeping enemies closer, but it's not germane—we hoped.) Kept them really close. Reminded them how they value to the communities we are collaborating with.

Lesson 13

I lost count of how many times somebody breathlessly reported: So-and-So is wealthy and perfectly positioned to step up for us. Or: I know somebody high up in a big foundation or a bigwig at a Fortune 500 corporation. (What's not to love about our friends, many of whom have good ideas and promising networks?) Of course, such out-of-the-blue prospects might someday bear fruit—but that's rarely, all too rarely, alas. And yet—and yet—we tracked down non-rabbit-hole leads wherever they took us.

Lesson 14

The mantra, explicit or implicit, for every nonprofit is *no money, no mission*. How true. How obvious. Every donated dollar mattered, because every gift is meaningful. No donation is too small. (Or, come on now, too large.) But why do people give to anything? Wrong question. People give to people, people with a vision that is inclusive of other people. You don't go to someone with hat in hand and expect them to metamorphose into Laureen Powell Jobs. (For the record, though, what's a chair without a dream? An ex-board chair?)

Lesson 15

People love stories. Everybody knows that. But the truth is deeper, more nuanced. That's because people are stories and stories are people. Speaking of which, here are two true stories you will be tempted not to believe, but they are stories that always inspired hope in me. A university alum every year sent in a donation of $600. Every year. Clockwork. $600. One year he sent in a check for $6,000,000. A high up-the-chain university administrator, a friend of mine, reached out to personally thank him and ask what inspired this unexpected largesse. "I wanted to see how you treated a $600 donor." True story. Here's another one. A nonprofit executive once met with a highly successful, progressive industrialist.

I know, admire, and trust them both. She solicited a donation of $10,000. He had studied the organization and was taken by its mission and people. He said he would not give $10,000. Instead, he would give $10,000,000. Which is what he did, and that's another true story. (Keep hope alive: our watchword.)

Lesson 16

Fundraising is about cultivating reciprocal relationships, about caring for your donors who care for your cause. Don't get this twisted. It's not about sending flowers or food baskets. I guarantee there is a generous donor who will be terminally irked their money was squandered on swag. (About hats, though, I carve out an exception, because hats with logos are cool and useful publicity when you are hiking and, if you search around, you can find a deal.)

Lesson 17

Writing a check is personal. And people give to success—as in delivering what was promised and what is urgently needed. So, make music. Make magic. We underscored success—not our organization's achievements with dollars raised or strategic planning or logo design or internal business, but the success experienced in the communities we worked with, thanks in significant part—and we stayed humble about this, too—to working with friends and colleagues who shared the vision and mission. Messaging is key. On this score, I take heart in the example of one famous person who gave away his worldly fortune to serve those in need of food, shelter, dignity: Francis of Assisi. He said, "Preach the gospel, if necessary use words." (Let's all get that tattoo.)

Lesson 18

In this dire epoch we are living in we naturally feel tempted to invoke the overused "now more than ever" principle. And what with this current administration ravaging nonprofits for diabolical sport, and what with economic uncertainty contaminating donors' moods and inclinations, our work is indeed called for now more than ever. There, just this one time I said it. After all, arts and education are almost always in resistance to the status quo, a challenge to the powers that be. We own it now more than ever.

Lesson 19

When would have been the perfect time to found New Literary Project? No idea if there is ever such a thing as perfect, but let me tell you what transpired one fateful day, Wednesday, June 10, 2015. That's when I hosted a gathering of friends and faculty of the English Department of the University of California, Berkeley, my grad school alma mater. The state has been struggling with drought for many years, as is well known. We could barely remember any precipitation the whole winter. But then, that late spring day in June, when even in droughtless years there was normally no rainfall, something amazing: it rained and rained and rained all day. Thrilling climate news, to be sure, not such great news for a party to be held outdoors. By five o'clock, though, as a hundred guests began to arrive, rain suddenly halted and clouds dramatically cleared. It morphed into a lovely, balmy, washed-clean blue sky California evening, pretty much perfect for a party. At that event, the incoming department chair was welcomed, Genaro Padilla. Speakers waxed eloquently, movingly, including Bob Hass, the poet laureate of the United States and Cal English professor, who read his poetry. The catered dinner was appropriately spectacular, my friend Peter Chastain (now of Via del Corso fame) outdoing himself (and from that day forward destined to become a stalwart NewLit supporter). Meanwhile, throughout the night, people talked, they came to know each other. Teachers and professors, artists and arts educators, community leaders, all connecting. There was a feeling in the emergent air that we could maybe make something new and meaningful involving teaching across the generations, a literary prize, a series of innovative outreach programs collaborating with heretofore sidelined communities. We did not have the entire picture at first, of course, but we kept talking. In the days following the party, a band of us commenced meeting and continued doing so throughout summer and fall, with Genaro as one of the leaders, and out of all this energy and fervor something new was being conceived—gradually taking on greater definition and eventually growing into what it is still becoming today. Looking back, you could even say we made it rain that day. And for the past ten years we haven't stopped making it rain NewLit ever since.

Lessons 20—to ∞

Despite the riven state of the country and the world—or maybe because we hoped to play a small part mending the fissures—we did all we could to make sure NewLit kept being re-born, welcoming new concepts, new programming, and most important, new people and new partners. Once upon a time, our small but mighty literary arts and education nonprofit may have been my brainchild, but it takes everybody to parent, to nurture, to foster a creation, to help it take its first steps and to teach it to speak out for itself, to help it adapt and learn, in order that it someday grow up and become what it means to be. On this score, a special moment resonates. I'll never forget a certain reading by some of the remarkable teenagers from our workshops, on one of our wildly animated public occasions. Afterward, an emotional father of one of the readers approached and said simply, with the conviction of love, "My daughter's life will never be the same." When I wake up in the middle of the night worrying, as I often did and as I still often do, I remember that I am not alone and, what's more, that the lives of people I may never meet may never be the same. Now ten years down the road, I know one life that will never be the same is my own. I also harbor the hope that, one day, another of those lives will belong to you.

—JOSEPH Di PRISCO

PART ONE

2025 JOYCE CAROL OATES PRIZES

Joyce Carol Oates Prize is named for the eminent author, an honorary member of New Literary Project's Board of Directors. The Prize is annually awarded to a mid-career author of fiction of major consequence, one who represents NewLit's vision and mission.

The Prize of $50,000 is given not for a specific book, but to a distinguished author who has emerged and is still emerging, and it is given in testament of literary achievement as well as in support of work to come.

NewLit thereby gratefully acknowledges Joyce Carol Oates's inspiring, lifelong impact as peerless teacher and writer, an author beloved and admired for generations by legions of students, writers, and readers around the country and the world. She embodies NewLit's commitments to literature, literacy, and opportunity.

For 2025, New Literary Project presents two prizes of $50,000 to:

Jennine Capó Crucet and Willy Vlautin

Previous JCO Prize Recipients:

2024 Ben Fountain

2023 Manuel Muñoz

2022 Lauren Groff

2021 Danielle Evans

2020 Daniel Mason

2019 Laila Lalami

2018 Anthony Marra

2017 T. Geronimo Johnson

It's hard for me to articulate just how much it means to me to win the 2025 Joyce Carol Oates Prize and to join the list of previous recipients—all writers whose work and careers I deeply admire and from whom I've learned so much. The best I can do for now is express my gratitude: Thank you to the New Literary Project and its Board of Directors, UC Berkeley, Saint Mary's College, and all their supporters and partners for the vital work they do in encouraging people to "write their hearts out" and for investing in writers at all stages of their careers. I cannot wait to join you all for the fall residency and be part of such a vibrant, nourishing community. Thank you to the jurors for selecting an incredible list of finalists; I'm honored to be among such stellar company. Thanks to each of the finalists for creating boldly and bravely, and much love to the incomparable Joyce Carol Oates, who leads us by example in that and other writerly realms. Thank you to every librarian, bookseller, and teacher out there, for their commitment to doing the hard work of keeping our hearts and minds open. I'm eternally grateful to my literary agent, Maria Massie, for her care and brilliance. I don't know where I'd be without her powerful faith in my work, her support, and her friendship. Oceans of gratitude to my editor, Tim O'Connell, for his superb editorial skills and for steadfastly believing in *Say Hello to My Little Friend* and its aims from the moment he first read it. Every writer should be so lucky as to have an editorial force like Tim in their corner. Thank you to the incredible Gina Mingacci, for all the doors she's opened (and wisely closed) and for her invaluable mentorship. My deepest thanks, always, goes to my family: to my beloved ancestors, for their wisdom, guidance, and protection; and to Esmé and Derek, for filling every single day with love, joy, and so much laughter. Without you two and the miracle of your love, there is no writing.

— Jennine Capó Crucet

"Jennine Capó Crucet is a writer who reminds us what words can do. Their power. Their unknowable mystery. She is a creator and a searcher for what is just, but she is also an entertainer, someone who understands inherently what happens when structure and imagination collide—that sacred space where language transforms and reaches back into the very soul of a place or a people or a culture. In *Say Hello To My Little Friend*,

Jennine blends two seemingly antipodal pillars of the American consciousness—Scarface and Moby Dick—to create an homage to the city of Miami. The novel, like the water that runs through it, touches on everything: Cuban immigration, the restacking of the American Dream, climate crises, Pitbull's musical canon, and one very intelligent killer whale, Lolita, whose all-seeing eye guides, consumes, and seeks justice, love, knowledge, freedom, and empowerment from the world that she has been cut off from. In combining these things, Jennine has done something I've never seen before, threaded a needle-sized needle with an orca-sized orca to tell the story of a city, its people, in a way that left me utterly slack jawed with her humor and brilliance. Thank you to the New Literary Project for selecting Jennine and *Say Hello to My Little Friend* for this remarkable honor. It's a work that inspires boldness, something she has done for her whole career and hopefully something with this acknowledgement she can engender in others."

—Tim O'Connell

Vice President, Editor, Simon & Schuster

I've been in love with the novel for most of my life. I was nineteen when I began working on my first one. I wasn't a great student, I had taken no writing classes, I just had a big edge to me and a wish to tell working class stories. Never once did I think I'd publish one or thirty-eight years later be fortunate enough to receive the Joyce Carol Oates Prize. When I heard this great news the first thing I thought of were my novels. They have been such great pals to me and have gotten me through a lot of hard years, so to be appreciated for them, well, I wanted to load them up in the car and take them out on the town for a serious night of celebration.

So much of recognition in art is luck and I've been a very fortunate man that way. I met my agent, Lesley Thorne, over twenty years ago at a gig I was playing. She's been a great advocate, friend, and champion of my books ever since. Amy Baker, my brilliant editor at HarperCollins, has always believed in working class fiction and has helped shape and focus my novels and has never once given up on them or let one of them fall through the cracks like so many novels do. I'm so grateful for her friendship and guidance. And my wife, Lee, who has put up with a man who plays 1960s Italian soundtrack records every day and lives inside other worlds for a living. She's the smartest, the toughest, and the coolest. My books and I are so honored and grateful for this recognition and to now be a part of New Literary Project.

—Willy Vlautin

"It was so exciting and rewarding to learn that Willy Vlautin is a recipient of the 2025 Joyce Carol Oates Prize. I've had the great pleasure and privilege of working with Willy for nearly twenty years over the course of seven published books (and counting). Through each of his remarkable novels, I've been impressed by the power of his words to deeply resonate, illuminate, and remain. I find myself still thinking about his characters, wondering how they're holding up in such difficult times, and hoping they're getting by. Willy has an extraordinary talent for confronting issues facing modern America. His novels cover themes including health care, homelessness, the housing crisis, the toll war takes on veterans and their families, addiction, mental health, loneliness, and regret. His portraits of everyday Americans are often heartbreaking, sometimes harrowing, but always hopeful, and they are bearable through the gentle care and respect he shows his characters and the resiliency of the human heart. Reading his work is an exercise in empathy and a lesson on how to be a better human being. I am so proud of willy for his dedication to telling these often difficult but necessary stories with unsentimental compassion, and I am so grateful to New Literary Project for honoring his body of work with this esteemed prize."

—Amy Baker
VP/Associate Publisher and Editorial Director, HarperCollins

AN EXCERPT FROM
SAY HELLO TO MY LITTLE FRIEND
JENNINE CAPÓ CRUCET

Taking place in 2017, Say Hello to My Little Friend *is a modern-day riff on* Moby Dick *set in my hometown of Miami, Florida, a city the most scientists predict will be underwater in our lifetimes. The novel follows Ismael Reyes—you can call him Izzy—as he fashions himself, for better or worse (spoiler alert: it's worse) after the character of Tony Montana in the film Scarface. His efforts soon lead him to the tank that houses Lolita, an orca held captive at the Miami Seaquarium, whose power—like the water surrounding her—permeates everything around her: from Miami's sinking streets, to Izzy's own memories, to the very heart of the novel itself. This excerpt is taken from the novel's opening. —JCC*

ETYMOLOGY

They were already on the water—twenty or so experienced sailors and divers and one biologist. They'd set out before sunrise in two speedboats loaded with explosives, along with a pilot and a scout in a seaplane overhead, which would prove crucial. These people were on a mission, and this story is as Miami as it gets, but like so many Miami stories—and there are so, so many worth telling—it really starts somewhere else and a long while back. This one begins on the gray waves of Penn Cove, all the way over in Washington State of all places, on August 8, 1970.

The goal that day was to capture several orca, preferably females, preferably juveniles, though it's likely those would be the only kind for which this crew could even try, seeing as how all orca, but especially adult males, are enormous. This kind of capture had been done before, but not by these sailors or this biologist. It was the kind of work that had a high turnover rate, as people could not, after doing it once, be induced by money or anything else to do what they'd done again. Which was partly why this time, with this contract, they were hoping for a larger haul: six or seven whales, if possible, and they were aiming for the lucky number.

That morning was cold despite the summer day—not a surprise, as the water there is freezing compared to what you get in Miami. There was fog; there was rain, but as the day went on it tapered, felt more like mist, then disappeared. The pod they were tracking and eventually chasing at some point split in two, and while the orca fooled the boats and the sailors—the family sent the children one way, with their mothers, while the rest led the boats in the opposite direction—they didn't fool the pilot for very long, and when the scout, binoculars pressed over eye sockets, saw what the orca had done—that they'd *devised a plan* to protect their young—he almost refused to radio down to the boats and give them their new location.

In the end, the sailors got seven, one being the wished-for juvenile female. The biologist with them estimated that this whale was between two and four years old. But estimate is just another word for guess: the truth is, no one outside of this orca's own family knows for sure how old she really is.

Ask the biologist: At what age is it safe to remove an orca from its mother? The biologist will shake her head and say, Whatever age it would be okay for you to lose yours.

Decades later, this whale remembers that morning well, still sometimes startles out of her half-sleep from the sound of the explosives used to divide them, or worse, from the piercing sensation of her mother's call—a memory but a sensation still—echoing over her from the other side of the sudden nets, from outside the floating pen in which she was trapped. She did not know how to get out. Her mother and aunts did not know how to get her and her cousins out. Those outside the pen stayed close and waited and panicked and blocked the boats and the ropes, the attempts to lasso them. They swam directly into the nets on purpose, hoping to tear them. They roughed up the water and spewed out every form of protest but in the end, their children were taken from them. She was the last of those captured to be lifted out of the ocean in a stretcher, the last one dragged onto land and into a vessel for transfer—a tank no bigger than her own body.

Five of their family died that day—drowned by the nets—their bodies sliced open and stuffed with rocks, anchors tied around their tails, lost, for a time, to the bottom of the sea. The others captured along with her all died within five years of that morning. What else could you call her survival but a miracle? What other word could you possibly use to describe it?

These aren't rhetorical questions.

One answer: you could just call it a fact. Or maybe, if you're trying to be funny: a fluke. Or maybe, in this case: the beginning of a legend.

Of her own beginnings—her first years in the ocean and not yet in a tank—she remembers everything, only some of those memories distorted by captivity: how she learned the sounds of her family, how she could speak with them before ever leaving her mother's body thanks to the other miracle of water. Of knowing too—without the help of sound and again thanks to water—where each of them was and what they were sensing, regardless of proximity. She knew their voices before their faces, felt their bodies within her own: facts that work like promises, sensations she still touches in her mind, the last reverberations of home that she absorbed as she was lifted out of the Salish Sea.

Here's another fact: the tiny tank situation didn't improve upon her forced relocation to Miami. She was given the name Lolita—whoever came up with it never read Nabokov and so didn't intend the allusion; they just thought the name sounded fittingly *tropical*—and has since lived in the smallest tank in the world.

And at first, she wasn't in there alone. Lolita—*so courageous and yet so gentle*, the veterinarian who chose her for the Miami Seaquarium said of her during the evaluation that preceded their offer to purchase her—joined the tank's current occupant, her adopted boyfriend-brother: a male orca known as Hugo, a whale not much older than her, captured three years earlier who would, in time, devote an entire afternoon to bashing his own head against the concrete walls of their tank in order to kill himself. That day's attempt—not his first—proved successful.

Lolita remembers that day too, and how she'd thought, at the sight of all that new blood in the water, at how this time, he no longer rose up for air: No, no, Hugo, *no*. But also: *Finally*. And also, to her terrified surprise, because she knew her kind were meant to live in families and did not know what this verdict meant for her own sanity: *Good riddance.*

Good riddance to the sound of his teeth gnawing against the edge of the tank. Good riddance to his bites, his swipes, his lunges at her and at their trainers. Good riddance to his circling and circling; to ten years of him taking up space in a tank too small for even just one of them; to his existence serving as a constant reminder of all she'd lost and of where she was not.

But that was years and years ago now.

She is still in that Miami tank, swims each day through the scene of his death. Hugo has been gone for close to four decades, replaced by dolphins in a misguided attempt to keep her company. She's grown used to their noise and can block out the nonsense of their language, learning to notice only the silence before they rake her with their teeth. But now there is this new noise, this rumble from the depths of this doomed city. Not another whale—no, definitely not—but a man, new to her. She hears something inside him, a precursor to his manhood, something that feels familiar, frighteningly—almost impossibly—like herself. When the tide is high and the water seeps into the city, as it does more and more each day, she thinks she can sometimes hear a call from the base of his brain, long-range and full of mourning and somehow still a child's, his cries—in a language she knows he's losing, the phrases indecipherable to her but their meaning known—hovering undetected in the hallways of his own memory.

The Lummi phrase for her kind means *our relations under the waves.* The Latin phrase means *of or belonging to the realm of the dead.*

Yes, inside him, there it is, the meaning almost a song: something he's forever letting go of, something he doesn't realize he's killed.

A BOSOM FRIEND

His name is Ismael Reyes, but almost everyone calls him Izzy. He considers the day he got the cease and desist letter from Pitbull's legal team the worst of his life, the reason being that his short-lived role as the number-one unauthorized Pitbull impersonator in the Greater Miami Area had actually been his best attempt at a life plan yet—or at least, the plan most likely to earn him enough easy extra money to move out of the townhouse he shared with his Tía Tere: his mother's sister, though he never thought of her that way, as he'd barely known his mother. Technically, despite by Miami standards maybe being a little old for the role, Teresa had played the part of Izzy's only parent since he was seven. And technically, it could be said that Izzy already lived on his own: in his Tía Tere's garage-turned-efficiency, with its own separate side entrance and his own key and everything; his only reasons for going into her part of the townhouse were if he had to use the kitchen or the bathroom or if he wanted to watch something on cable. The conversion of the garage into an almost-apartment was his high school graduation present, the mostly legal though definitely unpermitted construction project a gift from his Tía Tere, who'd recently begun praying that he'd move out soon so she could rent out the room to recoup its cost, hence her tacit endorsement of Izzy's cash-only Pitbull impersonator business plan. But that letter, written in some very official-sounding language, made it perfectly clear that Izzy's weekly photo ops at Dolphin Mall, his appearances at the Two-for-Tuesday happy hours at the Ale House down in Kendall, his standing near—but technically never in!—the entrances of several fading South Beach clubs: basically everything about his side hustle that had given him any recent hope about life after high school—and not being forever limited by the little he made working part-time at Don Shula's Hotel & Golf Club in Miami Lakes—had been deemed illegal. Copyright infringement, punishable with fines so large that the price tag of just an initial infraction was more than what he guessed his mother would've made in her entire life in Cuba, had she never tried to leave.

He was disappointed. Although not *Born and raised in the county of Dade* (only the latter being true), he'd committed to the daily shaving of his head to evoke the dull sheen of the real Pitbull's dome. He'd practiced the snarky giggle littering his lyrics, memorized all the words that rhymed with *culo*, invested in a well-tailored white blazer. On his drives to and from Don Shula's, he'd even made himself listen to Pitbull's latest album, the just-released *Climate Change*—the record didn't have a single hit on it despite having more featured artists than it did actual tracks—because he figured that was the record the real Pitbull would be trying to promote-slash-salvage after its disappointing mid-March debut, peaking at number 29 on the *Billboard 200*, pobrecito Pitbull. Point is:

Izzy really thought he made a good Pitbull. And he did, if he kept on his sunglasses—Izzy's eyes are brown, not blue. There was also the issue of his age and his height, as the real Pitbull is pushing forty and had maxed out at an angry five-seven, whereas Izzy has just turned the big Two-Oh and is blessed to have made it to five-eleven-and-a-half: great for Izzy's life in general but not-so-great for the Pitbull business. He'd charged less than he wanted and crouched down in photos for exactly those reasons—he was a reasonable guy! He imagined Pitbull to be one as well despite all the sonic evidence suggesting otherwise.

If only Izzy could just talk to him, cut through all the lawyers and shit, make his case man to man: that having a younger, better-looking version of yourself showing up in the Miami neighborhoods you list in almost every song would only elevate your quote-unquote brand; that Tía Tere lives for your remixes and is your biggest fan (not true at all, she thinks Pitbull is a hack and a clown, changes the station like a reflex whenever she hears his voice, but she did appreciate that Izzy had, prior to getting that letter, something relatively safe to do on weekends, something she wrote off as a strange but undeniable calling that also happened to earn him some cash); that imitation is the sincerest form of flattery or whatever; why do you even care, you're already rich as fuck; et cetera, et cetera. Izzy was sure he could change Pitbull's mind, maybe even end up in the background of a music video or something.

Alas, he understood from the letter that discussing the terms with the man himself was not an option, so the time had come for him to fully commit to his original life plan—the plan of his heart—to the idea that he'd dismissed as a fantasy a couple years earlier, as high school graduation loomed and as late-night movies on cable flooded over him from the one ancient and decidedly not-smart television in his Tía Tere's townhouse, a plan he'd reasoned away as probably too far-fetched and crazy-sounding, even by Miami standards (or at least, his experience of them; he can—and should!—thank his Tía Tere for the limits on *that* kind of knowing). He'd told himself his original plan was barely a plan at all, that it was more inherently dangerous and too ambitious, and why even go that route when he had in Pitbull an innocuous enough Mr. 305 turned Mr. Worldwide, a quote-unquote rapper who was really just a barely bilingual auto-tuned businessman ticking off the Latino box on the commercial music industry's checklist for crap with a resounding *Dah-leh*? But with Pitbull himself having weighed in on Izzy's future, he could see the ways he'd underestimated himself, how he'd denied himself the pleasure of taking his cues from his real hero. He could no longer follow that easier path, as he had—right in front of him—his message from Pitbull-slash-the Universe-slash-the black-and-white image scowling at him from the movie poster on the wall across from his bed. The time had come for him to accept his destiny, to believe that the world really could be his, to embrace his Cuban birth and his huge balls; he would re-make himself into Tony Montana for the new millennium, Miami's modern-day Scarface.

What this meant immediately: he could let his hair grow back, which was a huge relief, as no twenty-year-old should play at being bald when nature hasn't forced it on him. It meant he needed his very own Manolo, a guy to follow him around and hopefully do most of the boring but necessary stuff largely behind the scenes. It meant—if he really wanted to be authentic here—that he would need to quit his crappy job at Don Shula's in order to get a crappier job as a dishwasher in a Little Havana restaurant, a job that he and his Manolo would eventually quit once shadier shit was in the works. It meant he needed to practice saying *hello to his little friend* and ramping up his usage of the word *fuck*. He needed a pet tiger and a Michelle Pfeiffer, but really, if he wanted to avoid falling short this time, he needed to start out aiming higher: he needed something better than a tiger or a Pfeiffer—a more dangerous pet and/or lady. He needed *Super* Manolo. Because Izzy's mistake with the Pitbull route was that he'd tried to become that man rather than surpass him. This time, with this plan, he would have to surpass even what he could not yet imagine.

He needed to watch the movie again, probably.

So no, despite what Izzy thinks, the day that brought the letter killing his first American Dream was not the worst day of his life, not by a long shot. Technically, that day is both already behind him and also hanging ahead of him, the memory and possibility of it already sensed—somehow—by Izzy's Better-Than-a-Tiger: Miami's favorite and only captive orca, known here as Lolita, this sinking city's whale, simmering in the too-warm water of her tank, ever-circling the concrete, hoping and waiting for him.

LOOMINGS

What else does Lolita know? It might feel impossible to imagine, but why not try: she knows she's in Miami, Florida, but that she's not from here, that such a thing is impossible. She knows roughly the location of her still-living family members—and so, of her mother—though this is less known than felt, which is the case for much of what you'd call *knowing*. She knows *Lolita* is just a stage name, a character, not the name she was born into but it's the one to which she's long answered. She knows, roughly, her age, that she has been in this tank for several decades, that her rituals around each sunrise have helped her keep track of the passage of long time—and so she knows the year is 2017, though she doesn't use that number to mark it: you can't know what number she holds in her mind—how could you?—only that it's much larger, maybe a different shape. She knows her show times. She knows that people like the water even though for her it's too warm—and so she does her best to drench the crowd every day, twice a day. Why not? It seems to her that it takes very little to make people happy, and when people feel happy, she knows it: she can, at times, sense that joy directly in the minds of those still too young to have achieved coherent speech (a phenomenon likely attributed to the paralimbic region of her brain; in the ocean, this structure would've allowed her to communicate with members of her pod without any sound at all—the best word for that, given the limits of this language, being *telepathy*). She knows she is the Most Important Thing at the Seaquarium, and she knows—somehow—that *Seaquarium* is not a real word. She knows—no, be accurate: knows *of*—LeBron James and him taking his talents to South Beach, though he and his talents were actually in Downtown Miami, across from her tank on Virginia Key, meaning: not South Beach at all. She knows South Beach is, for now, three or so feet above sea level. She knows something is wrong with the warming water and with the ground, and that it feels like a sinking—but no, it's the water rising from the limestone below to meet her; she thinks maybe this is part of some greater plan to get her out of that tank, but of this she can't be sure. She knows only that something is rippling that was not rippling before, not at this rate or at this amplitude, that the sound of it comes and goes with the tides, and so every day she listens for as far as she can listen, swaying her fat-filled jawbone in and out of the water when her trainers believe her to be resting. And it's in this listening that she hears Izzy, halfway across the city, wondering while he showers where the fuck he's going to find a Manolo and a Pfeiffer and, eventually, something like her.

THE HUNT BEGINS

Izzy decides to start with interviews. He knows he needs to watch the movie again—he knows, he knows—but for now he thinks he can move forward on the Manolo front without a refresher. Granted, Tony Montana already knew the real Manolo from their lives in Cuba; in the movie, Tony didn't need to go searching for his Manolo, but Izzy figures that when you're crafting yourself into Scarface, the only way to dive in is to accept where you're at, then move the right pieces into place so that the money, then the power—and after that the women, according to the film's stated logic—can eventually flow your way. He pulls down his high school yearbook from the bookshelf where there isn't a single other book and turns to the back, to where people signed it. Most of the signers were women, but there were three guys—he counts them; two are named Rudy—and it is these three fellow Hialeah Lakes High grads who have, the way he figures it, an automatic berth into the Manolo Interview Round.

He looks up each guy on Instagram—but doesn't follow them, as that would make him seem like a try-hard—and shows their pictures to his Tía Tere, asking her what she knows and claiming he's looking to reach out and make friends, something she half-heartedly reminds him to do *in real life* whenever she sees him looking at his phone. His Tía Tere knows people, is basically the central spoke in her network of *cubanas metidas*, their headquarters being the Sedano's Supermarket on Palm Avenue where they buy their lottery tickets. Every area-Cuban of a certain generation knows Teresa and her story, which is also Izzy's story: how she took in her nephew after his mother drowned trying to cross over, how she'd raised him as her own—even though she'd never wanted kids herself, she liked to remind people. If his Tía Tere didn't know someone directly, she knew their mother or their tía or their madrina, so within half an hour Izzy has a workplace and a cell number for each guy. He considers texting them but decides to show up at their jobs instead; he wants to see them in action, *in real life*, but more importantly, he figures catching them by surprise is what Tony Montana would do, and given that hunting for a Manolo already strays from—or perhaps predates—the literal *Scarface* plot, Izzy wants to do whatever he can to start this shit off right.

The first one, the one not named Rudy, works at Pembroke Lakes Mall all the way up in Broward, at the T-Mobile stand right near the food court. It would be a better sign if he worked for Verizon or AT&T, but whatever, dude's got to start somewhere, right? Irregardless of any cease-and-desist letter, you can't just start off as Mr. Worldwide, not without first spending some time as Mr. 305.

Not-a-Rudy (his name is Geovany) looks exactly the same as he does in his yearbook photo. Same shitty block of a beard hiding a weak chin, same fade, same too-big-to-be-real diamond studs in his earlobes. He's even wearing a tie like in the picture, though this one is T-Mobile pink instead of the standard-issue black ones they sling around your neck when you sit for your senior year portraits. The only thing maybe different about him is his neck, which is for sure thicker, Izzy thinks. Or maybe just stronger.

—Wassup, chico, Izzy says, the endearment a holdover from his Pitbull act. He slaps forearms with the guy across the stand's counter and adds, It's been a minute.

—Ernie! the guy says. What happened to your hair, dog? Coño, look at you, you're fucking diesel.

—It's Izzy, bro. Ismael.

Izzy definitely lifts but doesn't consider himself *diesel* by any means. He barely thinks of himself as *ripped*, maybe on his way to *jacked*, which is, as far as he understands, still a couple levels shy of *diesel*. Is it Izzy who doesn't see himself accurately, or is this guy bad at sizing people up? If it's the latter, shouldn't that disqualify this guy from being a potential Manolo, given that sizing people up is probably an integral part of the job? Plus, the guy misremembered Izzy's name: not exactly good signs, not that he thinks he's looking for any.

Then by way of apology the guy says *Coño, fuck me, my bad* like three times, so Izzy considers him back in the running: he already has the vocabulary. He's got a break coming up, so they make plans to meet at the Sbarro in four, maybe five minutes.

Izzy sits with his back to the heat-lamped pizza glistening behind the sneeze guard to keep from buying all the slices. Thinking about rubbing his still-bald head with the garlicked grease pooling in each cheesy pizza crater also sort of works to keep him from wanting it. He wants to think that his days of consuming cheap mall garbage are as of right then literally behind him. Already he feels on his way to being too powerful to waste time thinking about something as basic as food. He can't remember if the movie ever shows Tony Montana actually eating anything other than cocaine.

Six or seven minutes later, the guy sits down across from him, a Diet Coke in his fist. He spreads his knees so far apart they knock away the empty seats on either side of him and says, Are you fucking 'roiding, bro? They say that shit shrinks your nuts but only if you do it like, *a lot* a lot.

—Nah, bro. I don't mess with that shit.

—You sure? You interested though? No pressure, whatever, how you been?

—Good, good. Busy. I'm trying to be like the next Scarface.

—Like the rapper? *My mind is playin' tricks on me!* I didn't know you could rap!

—No, like *Scarface* Scarface. Like the original. Tony Montana, like *her womb is so polluted.*

The guy leans back and says, Sorry to tell you and not for nothing, but you aren't Scarface material, bro. Like *at all*, if you're asking me. Which you basically are and I say you can't pull that shit off.

—Coño, bro. I'm *not* asking you. I'm looking for a Manolo.

—You know you sorta look like Pitbull with your head shaved like that? Except for the eyes, the guy says, smoothing down his tie. Fucking brown eyes wrecks it.

The guy spins his phone on the table between them.

—Oh cuz you're such big shit, working at T-Mobile. Can't even get a job at a real place like Verizon.

—Fuck you, bro, the fuck you even doing with your life?

—I just told you. I need a Manolo.

—*What?* I ain't no fucking Manolo! The guy grabs his phone and shoves it in his front pocket, then points at Izzy with sideways gun fingers. You'd be my fucking Manolo if anything, freaking ESL motherfucker. Remember back in middle school, you still had that ref accent in math saying *pa-ra-BO-la* instead of *pa-RA-bo-la*? Straight up Manolo shit right there, he says with a good tug on his crotch.

Izzy stands up and says, Oh you think so? Whatever, I did better than *you* in that class, so fuck that. He flexes his pecs, feels his traps engage along the ridge of his shoulders and the sides of his neck, making himself as big as he can. Fucking weak-ass motherfucker. Do you even lift, bro?

The guy doesn't stand up. He just sits there and laughs, rolling his Diet Coke can between the palms of his hands. Izzy tosses a crumpled-up napkin on the floor and stomps away.

—The fuck is your problem? the guy says to the chairs Izzy's shoved out of his way. Coño bro, you always seemed a little sad back in the day but you know what? Get as ripped as you want, doesn't matter, your fucking head's still *off*.

The guy points his gun-fingers to his own skull, but Izzy doesn't see it. He's cutting across the food court, trying to tune the guy out, but he can't help it: he hears the guy yell, Good luck, Manolo!

Izzy drives to the gym straight from the mall, deciding he needs to lift for a while before finding the next guy, the first Rudy. He has never taken steroids, but as he watches his arms and chest flex in the mirror wall, he wonders if the dough of his high school fat somehow absorbed steroids through the sweat of the guys around him. Maybe he hasn't been wiping off the machines so well. He thinks of garlic knots and imagines himself swallowing them whole but not digesting them: instead, each greasy lump magically migrates to his biceps, bolstering the muscles from underneath, the crusts pushing up his skin like some kind of bread-based implants. He benches ten pounds more than he's ever done, thinking not of the danger of carbs, but of what else they could come to mean: forbidden blasts of energy, quick and undeniable power.

KING TIDE

It doesn't rain while Izzy is inside the gym, and as he leaves, there isn't a cloud in the sky; the clouds don't roll in from the Everglades until later in the day, the heat and humidity and pressure summoning them from the west each afternoon, the storms they bring controlling the rhythms of Miami life with more force than any clock or rush-hour traffic pattern. And yet a puddle of what is definitely water surrounds his car as if it had poured for the last hour. The water was there when he arrived, but he didn't notice it as he got down from the car, the puddle small and oily enough earlier that he'd just parked over it, assuming it had leaked out of some other car's engine. Now he has to lunge across what looks like a custom-made moat, straddling a couple feet of water and leaping into his front seat to keep his sneakers dry.

All around the city this is happening more and more, water seeping up from the ground: sunny day flooding. Izzy doesn't call it that, or know that others call it that, or know the terrifying science/magic behind it, how—because it's connected to the tides—even the moon is involved. This city is, for him, just kind of wet all the time, and yeah, maybe it's worse than it used to be. Every time he has to cross over a sudden puddle like this, he figures a storm just passed, a quick one he just must've missed or didn't notice—what else could it be? He doesn't want to think about it. Besides, he's been doing splits over puddles since his first days in Miami. So many memories of his Tía Tere taking him to school and driving super slow so as not to make a wake, her Corolla floating over floods bumper-high after even the quickest and slimmest of rain showers: the water in the ground even back then was already so high it couldn't take on a drop more.

It's this water that is coming for him, for his Tía Tere's townhouse, for almost everyone's homes, starting with the septic tanks, many of which are failing. It's an inevitability: every septic tank in this city will fail. Because they are slowly being submerged. And there's no way to (legally) put those houses on the public sewer system if they aren't already: already, to dig down in those neighborhoods is to hit water before you get deep enough to lay new pipes. It's why the city of Miami Beach raised the roads by a few feet, buying themselves another decade or two of tourism. It's why the first dozen floors of every new building downtown—buildings with owners who live in other countries, all taking out huge insurance policies waiting to be cashed in with the next big hurricane—are dedicated to parking. It's why there are roaches everywhere in this city, inside every home no matter how often you clean it or have it cleaned, no matter how much pesticide you ring those homes in—those *fucking cockroaches* that Scarface curses by name are just trying to stay above that rising water line. The roaches, the ants, the palmetto bugs, the garter snakes, the green and brown anoles, the geckos, the toads, the salamanders, the various kinds of termites, even the opossums sometimes: they have no other choice but to come inside to stay dry. More and more, and for now—and depending on the moon and the time of day, month, year—inside your house is the safest place, because yes, they can float, maybe even tread water for a while, but unlike other creatures in this city, they aren't designed to swim forever. They're coming inside because they want to survive: they are all, like Lolita in her tank (though given what the floods could theoretically mean for her, she shares little of their trepidation), listening to the water coming up from the ground, to the future glimpsed when it's at its highest. To the promise of what it will reclaim.

AN EXCERPT FROM
THE HORSE
WILLY VLAUTIN

Al Ward, a journeyman musician and the main protagonist of The Horse, *is a damaged man and in my experience damaged people tend to attract damaged people both in romance and in friendship. In this excerpt Al and his girlfriend, a waitress named Maxine, fall in love. Both walk on the edge of life but in each other, at least for a while, they find stable ground. —WV*

[From Chaper 10]

They had lived together five months when Maxine came home from work and said, "I have a present for you." Al was sitting at the kitchen table. The Telecaster was in his lap and a spiral notebook sat open in front of him. "Can you take off for a week starting tonight?"

"Sure," he said. "Why?"

"We're going on vacation."

"Where?"

"You'll see, but we'll be gone five days and we gotta leave pretty soon."

She told him to pack a bag and bring his guitar, a swimsuit, and river shoes. In the trunk was her own suitcase, a cooler, and two sacks of groceries. Al loaded his things and Maxine drove them less than a mile to River House Motor Hotel, where she had reserved a deluxe suite for five nights.

The room was on the second floor and Chinese-themed, with white shag carpet and traditional landscape paintings of villages and forests and bridges on the walls. The light fixtures were faux paper lamps, the bedspread was white with Chinese writing on it, and the furniture was glossy black painted with bright l flowers. The bathroom had both a tub and a walk-in shower large enough for two people. On the balcony were two chairs and a table that looked over the Truckee River. Al leaned against the railing and looked east, thirty yards down the river, to where he and Vern had gone swimming years before. He pointed to the hundred-year-old cottonwood tree that stood on the bank. "Did I ever tell you my uncle Vern and I used to hang out under that tree?"

"You told me," Maxine said, and leaned on the railing next to him.

"Did you get us the room here because of that?"

"Yeah."

Al went to her and kissed her and tears welled in his eyes and he told her he loved her. They went to bed with the balcony door open and the sound of the river rushing past. In the room they drank and fucked for two days and left only to eat. On the third day Maxine went back to her job at Franco's and Al stayed behind. When afternoon came, he walked to the restaurant and picked her up. On the way back he bought two bottles of Orange Crush and they changed into their swimsuits and swam in the same deep pool underneath the same cottonwood tree that he and Vern had twenty years before. On warm river rocks they sat and Maxine's hair was wet and she wore a blue bikini and Converse tennis shoes and sunglasses. She sat cross-legged and held the Orange Crush in her hand and looked out at the Mapes and Cal Neva casinos.

"Can I tell you something, Al?"

"Sure," he said.

"I just…I just want you to know that deep down I always knew I'd get lucky. That someday I wouldn't be alone. That I wouldn't always feel so alone. I didn't know when it would happen, but I knew somehow it would. I just never imagined it would take this long or that I'd…that I'd get so ruined along the way. That I'd get so hopeless. I remember when I was living in that car in Florida. Sometimes I'd just curl in a ball and say to myself, 'My lucky time will come. My lucky time will come.' I'd say it over and over. And I really tried to believe it. Believe that someday, somehow, a door would open a little bit and I'd be smart enough to walk through it, and once I did, I'd be different. I'd be…I haven't been great in life, Al. I've been with people and done things that make me so sad that I've just wanted to give up and die. I'm not playing around when I say that. I…But now…" She looked at him and smiled. "Now I'm nothing more than a part-time ledge walker."

"A ledge walker?"

"Just walking on the edge of things. Always one or two steps from jumping off. For the last few years, before I met you, I'd been walking that edge closer, you know?"

"Yeah."

"You do know, don't you?"

"I felt that way most of my life."

"That's why I'm telling you. Because you understand what it means to be so close to giving up that all it takes is one more step. But I'm not going to take that step. Because for me, the door I was talking about has finally opened and I'm not gonna stay scared or hate myself. I'm going to go through it because on the other side is you . . . I don't care if I'm making a mistake saying all this. Or if it causes you to run away. I'm just so tired of walking the ledge that I'm gonna give everything to you. Everything I have . . . Did I ever tell you about my uncle Sailor? He was a cowboy who worked a ranch outside of Elko."

"I don't think so. How did he get the name Sailor if he was a cowboy?"

Maxine wiped her eyes and took a drink of the Orange Crush. "When he was young, he went to San Francisco and got drunk with some sailors on shore leave. They all got tattoos, so he did, too. He got a big one of a woman on his forearm, a sailor pinup girl. He also got HOLD on his right knuckles and FAST on his left. I guess that means not to give up, not to ever let go of the rope. Everyone at home made fun of him because no one back there had tattoos. They began calling him Sailor and the name stuck . . . Years later, he broke his leg getting bucked off a horse, and he lived with us. He was my dad's little brother and he was maybe thirty and had a huge cast on his leg. All day long he just sat on our porch and sucked on lemon drop candies and listened to the radio. Sometimes I'd walk by and he'd be just sitting there so sad-looking. I don't know why he was so sad, but even as a kid I could feel it. I really could. In his own way I think he was a ledge walker. My mother said he was the loneliest man she'd ever met. When he healed, he went back to the ranch, but eight months later he had bad luck again. This time a horse kicked out when he was shoeing it and he broke three ribs. My dad gave him money so he would stay in a motel in Elko and not with us. It all seemed so hopeless for him... And then... And then he met a maid named Gladys.

She cleaned his room and they fell in love. I'm serious. They did. They got married and… You know, they came and visited us a few times and they were really happy. They loved each other and…they…they got lucky, Al. He was saved because he walked through the door."

A jet flew overhead and left a long lazy contrail across the blue sky. Cars and trucks went across the Lake Street Bridge and the sun began to disappear behind the Sierras. Maxine put her feet in the river water and set her empty bottle on the rock.

"You know for years I've been getting more and more lost in my head. It's like swimming farther and farther out. Getting so alone and hopeless that I was almost certain there was no way I could ever get myself back. I don't know why I do it. I really don't. But I just wake up in the morning and keep swimming farther out. Do you know what I mean?

"Yeah, I know," Al whispered.

"Ledge walking and swimming." She laughed and dropped into the river. Only her head stuck out of the water and she looked at him and smiled. "But you saved me from the sea, Al. You saved me from swimming so far out that I would never be able to get back…. I know it's a gamble telling you all this. I've been waking up in the middle of the night worrying about telling you. About me ruining everything. But I'm tired of always losing things because I care about them. And Jesus, I'm tired of being scared. I just love you so much I had to tell you. I love you so much I can't help but tell you."

The last day at the River House, Al walked Maxine to work and afterward he went to Premier pawnshop on Virginia Street and bought her a gold wedding band. He bought a bottle of champagne from a liquor store and went to the duplex, put on his best suit, his best shirt, and boots, and walked back to Franco's and waited across the street until Maxine got off work. He gave her the ring outside the Mapes Casino in the fading warm afternoon light. They celebrated with a drink at the Sky Room and two hours later were married at the Park Wedding Chapel.

But then thinking of Maxine was like a drink itself. Heaven and relief that soon disappeared into sickness and regret, sorrow and self-hatred. He looked out the window and the worry over the horse came back and the week at the River House and the songs he'd written for Maxine and their time together disappeared. "River House #3,"

"Saved from the Sea," "Waking Up in a Chinese Room," "Me and My Maxine," "Living in a Car in Florida," "The Ballad of Sailor & Gladys," "Drifting Out Past the Breakers," "Crown Royal and a King-Size Bed," "Maxine Don't Go Fading," "Our Clothes Were in a Pile on the Floor," "The Lost Week," "Sleeping by the River," "The Cottonwood Tree," "The Week Time Stopped," "Swimming Under Casino Lights," A Girl Floating on a River," "I Can't See the Shore," "Hold Fast," "Walking That Ledge," "Maxine #6," "The Girl and the Bartender from New Orleans," "The Woman with a Scar That Never Healed," "I Didn't Know Where I Ended and Where You Began."

AN EXCERPT FROM
DON'T SKIP OUT ON ME
WILLY VLAUTIN

I wrote Don't Skip Out On Me *after seeing too many broken kids, kids that were never given a chance, that weren't loved enough, that were somehow cast aside or forgotten. The old man, Mr. Reese, has been trying to help his ranch hand, Horace, find his way into adulthood. In this excerpt Mr. Reese is driving home after watching Horace fight in a Golden Gloves boxing tournament to find two hobo kids and their dog huddled in the bed of his truck. These wayward drifters are treating their dog the way they've been most likely treated. Mr. Reese is both trying to understand the boys and help a dog in distress. —WV*

Chaper 13

Mr. Reese stopped at a service station in Wendover. As he got gas, he noticed his truck's back right tire was low. He moved the truck to the edge of the station, in near darkness, and filled the tire from a coin-operated air compressor. After that he went inside, bought a cup of coffee and a donut, and got back on the road. He listened to the radio and jumped stations as the night gave them and took them away. Interstate 80 led to 93 and soon he was on a desolate desert road where no traffic passed.

An hour outside of Ely he felt movement in the bed of the truck and pulled to the shoulder and parked. From the glove box he took a flashlight and got out. He checked the tires and then looked underneath the truck, but everything seemed normal. As he stood back up, he saw the taut canvas tarp covering the bed move. He unfastened one of the tailgate corners to find two boys lying flat, surrounded by his supplies.

"What are you two doing back here?" he said, startled.

"Nothing," one of the boys said.

"Both of you get out of there now," Mr. Reese said and unclasped three more hooks and pulled back the canvas. The boys stood up in the bed and then jumped down onto the side of the road. The bigger of the two was holding a dog, a medium-sized black mutt, in his left arm, and set it on the ground. A choke chain hung around its neck and a rope ran from it to the boy's belt. The mutt sat in the dirt and began licking at its right paw.

Mr. Reese ran the flashlight over them. The bigger of the two looked to be in his late teens and was tall and heavy. The other boy seemed younger and was too thin, and even in the poor light he looked anemic, his face sallow. Both had scraggly beards and wore cut-offs and thin black T-shirts. Mr. Reese looked in the bed of the truck and saw two backpacks with sleeping bags attached to them.

"Where you two trying to get to?"

"Mexico," the bigger of the two said.

"Where in Mexico?"

"Los Mochis."

Mr. Reese shook his head. "How did you know which way I was going?"

"We didn't. We were just sick of waiting."

"Don't you know you could get shot doing something like this?"

They just looked at him.

"How much water do you guys have?"

"Half a gallon, maybe," the bigger said.

Mr. Reese again shook his head. "It's supposed to be over a hundred tomorrow and there's nothing out here, no shade of any sort. Did you think of that?"

The two kept silent.

Mr. Reese paused and then kicked the ground. "I can't see you two getting a ride this late and who knows about tomorrow, so I'll give you a ride as far as Ely and then you're out, okay?"

The two nodded.

"Get in the bed the way you were and I'll put the canvas back."

The bigger grabbed the leash and yanked the dog off the ground by its neck, choking him, until he pulled him into his arms. The smaller boy got in the bed of the truck, took the dog, and then the bigger boy got in.

They both laid flat and Mr. Reese rehooked the canvas tarp and got on the road again.

In Ely he parked at the Silver State Restaurant and unclasped the canvas cover. The smaller boy jumped down first and the bigger handed him their backpacks and the dog. Mr. Reese looked over his supplies, glanced inside the cooler, and when he was satisfied nothing had been taken pulled the canvas back over the bed.

It was past midnight. The two boys stood looking around. The smaller of the two said in a stuttering voice, "Wha…Wha…What's the nearest town…af…aft…after here?"

"There's not much," Mr. Reese said and took off his glasses and cleaned them on his shirt. "You're pretty far away from anything. But if you're heading south, I'd say Las Vegas. It's three or four hours away, depending."

"Is…Is…Is it hot in Las…Las Vegas too?"

"This time of year it's hot over the entire area, and it will be for a while." Mr. Reese looked at the dog where it stood next to the bigger boy. There was goop in its eyes, it wasn't putting weight on its front right paw, and he could see its ribs even in the darkness. He looked back to the boys. "Are you two hungry?"

They glanced at each other and nodded.

Mr. Reese pointed to the front door of the restaurant. "I'll buy you guys some chow if you want."

The older of the two tied the dog to a bike rack near the entrance and they went inside. The restaurant was empty but for a fat middle-aged waitress, who led them to a rectangular table in the middle of the room. The boys leaned their backpacks against the edge of the table and sat opposite Mr. Reese. Under the fluorescent lights they looked even worse. Their clothes were dirty and threadbare, and their hair was cut crudely, long in places, short in others. Both had acne, some pimples red and bursting, others scabbed over. They smelled. The smaller of the two chewed his nails and sat hunched over as the waitress brought water and menus. They both ordered full turkey dinners and Cokes. Mr. Reese ordered a cheeseburger and a cup of coffee.

"So, what are your names?" he asked after the waitress left.

"People call me Captain and he's Bob," the bigger of the two said.

"Why aren't you in school?"

They both shrugged.

"What's your dog's name?"

"N…N…" Bob tried.

"Knife," said Captain.

"What's wrong with his paw?"

"He cut it on something."

"What about his eyes?"

They again both shrugged and the waitress came back with their drinks.

Bob looked at Mr. Reese. "He's…He's got worms…worms coming out of his ass."

"All he does is scratch all night," Captain said and drank off his soda. Mr. Reese put sugar in his coffee. "Do you have any idea how bad you both smell? You can shower in truck stops. They have showers and laundry facilities at most of them."

The two boys looked at each other and smiled.

Mr. Reese took a drink of coffee. "Why are you going to Mexico?"

"Why do you care?" said Captain.

"I'm just curious, more than anything," Mr. Reese said.

"I'm just trying to understand. I figure I gave you a ride, didn't leave you stranded, didn't call the police and I'm buying you dinner. The least you could do is answer a few questions."

"We…We…We know some people there. We can live on the beach," Bob said and again chewed his nails.

"But isn't Los Mochis nine or ten hours from the border?"

They shrugged their shoulders.

"You don't know?"

Neither said anything.

"What kind of work can you get down there?"

"We ain't going down there to work," said Captain.

"How you gonna eat?"

"You don't have to work to eat," he scoffed and then got up from the table and walked to the bathroom. Bob kept his head down and drank sip after sip of soda until he had finished it.

"Where'd you get all those tattoos?" Mr. Reese asked.

"Lo…Lots of diff…different places," he said. On his left hand was a black pistol and three crude Xs around it. On his right were four Xs and a red-and-black cardinal that seemed the only professional tattoo. On his wrist was a rudimentary cross and above it read "R.I.P. JO 9-23-15."

"Do you understand Spanish?"

Bob shook his head.

"How about your friend?"

He shrugged his shoulders.

"They only speak Spanish in Mexico, and they use different money down there."

"Different money?"

Mr. Reese nodded. "They use the peso. How old are you?"

"Six…Six…Sixteen."

The waitress came then, set the food down, and Bob began eating. She refilled his soda and Captain came from the bathroom and sat back down.

"She already got you another one?" he asked.

Bob nodded and Captain took his glass, drank it in two swallows and began eating.

Mr. Reese watched the boys as he ate. "I know you don't want to talk to an old man, but out of curiosity I have to ask, what sorta plan do you guys have for your future?"

They looked at him but didn't answer.

"Don't you want to have your own place to live in? Get a car, have your own money, a family someday?"

The boys looked at each other, again smiled, but said nothing. They just kept eating. Bob finished half his plate and pushed it away, so Captain took it, scraped the remains onto his own plate and began eating them. The waitress came and refilled both of their drinks again.

"Are your families worried about you?"

Captain just shook his head.

"My…mom's worried," Bob said.

"But his mom's so fat she can't even get out of her bed. She's so big she's stuck in there. People have to come just to help her use the can."

Bob nodded timidly and the waitress set down the bill. Captain asked for another refill on his soda and the waitress came back with a full glass and Mr. Reese paid her. When Captain finished the drink, they left. Mr. Reese followed the boys outside and watched as they put on their backpacks.

"I have a proposition," he said and took out his billfold.

"I want to buy your dog off you for fifty bucks." He held the money out so they could see it. "He's in rough shape; you must have noticed that. He can't stand on his right paw and his eyes are infected. He's underweight and you said he has worms. And you won't be able to get him across the border. Most likely they won't let you. Even if you can, it'll be harder for you to catch rides with a dog. My wife and I live on a ranch. He'll have a good life with me."

Captain looked at Mr. Reese. "How about you throw in the cooler too?"

"I can't do that," he said. "No, fifty is what I have to spend. Fifty is the offer."

Captain didn't look at Bob or the dog. He only nodded.

Mr. Reese gave him the money and Captain unhooked the leash from around his belt and handed it to the old man. "How about you give us a ride to Las Vegas?"

"I can't do that either," Mr. Reese said. "I'm not going that way."

Captain shook his head, and without saying anything the two of them began walking away.

WHY IS YOUR WRITING SO VIOLENT?
A Familiar Question
JOYCE CAROL OATES

When people say there is too much violence in my books, what they are saying is there is too much reality in life.

It was on a chill but sunny May morning in 1980 in an antiquated auditorium of steeply tiered seats at the University of Warsaw that the question was asked of me by an earnest young man of about twenty-five, who, like most of the Poles we met, spoke excellent English: Why was my writing so violent? Might it be that my "personal experience," "perhaps my childhood," and, in any case, my "unique temperament" had so "distorted" my vision of mankind and of history that the fiction of "Joyce Carol Oates" represented only an "extreme attitude," unfortunately prevalent in contemporary American literature?

That this familiar question was asked of me in Warsaw, where in September of 1944 the insurrection against the Germans by the Polish underground had begun, with the eventual consequence that 200,000 Poles were slaughtered; that this question was asked of me in a city blown up by the departing German Army (the Red Army having discreetly paused on the banks of the Vistula to allow five weeks of destruction before crossing to "liberate" what remained of Warsaw); that it was asked of me with a hint of reproach that clearly resonated throughout the crowded gathering struck me as so painful and so ironic and so dispiriting and, in a sad way, so amusing that I could only offer some judiciously chosen and diplomatic words in response.

"Why do you focus on the violent?" The question was asked in Oslo, in Helsinki, in Brussels, in Budapest and in that dramatically "Western" city in Eastern Europe known for its encircling wall. In West Berlin the question was asked with great courtesy and tact, not many miles from where Adolf Hitler proclaimed the Second World War and Dr. Goebbels advanced the notion of "total war." This time the question came with the thoughtful addendum that perhaps my "vision" as a "novelist" had been much influenced by the fact that I had lived for many years in Detroit, Michigan (which appears to have the reputation throughout the world of being a "violent city.")

"You had an unhappy childhood, Miss Oates?"—asked with quizzical smiles, some measure of pity, sympathy. "You were often frightened by life?"

What are we to make of the stubborn bitter truth that one's legitimacy is judged by whether one appears to be "happy" or "unhappy"; that one's work is somehow assessed in terms of the spiritual uplift it offers? "Happiness" is predicated as a cultural norm, so that any deviation from it, however justified, however inescapable, arouses not only pity but reproach. As true as this might be for male writers, it is all the more true for female writers, since there is a violation of some unspoken rule in the very fact that a woman writes—that is, thinks.

It was once put to me directly, and no doubt has often been suggested by indirection, that I should focus my writing on "domestic" and "subjective" material, in the manner (for instance) of Jane Austen or Virginia Woolf, that I should leave large social-philosophical issues to men. The implication is that if Jane Austen and Virginia Woolf had lived in Detroit, they might have been successful in "transcending" their environment and writing novels in which not a hint of "violence" could be detected. Woolf might have been tremulous, quivering with sensitive insights, and not distracted by the vicissitudes of the world around her; Austen might have been arch and amusing and "delightful," and fit to be read by virtually anyone. If they successfully resisted writing about large "social issues" in their own times, it is implied, surely, they would not have failed in this new and challenging context, and "femininity" would not have to be despoiled.

The question is always insulting. The question is always ignorant. The question is always sexist. We seem to have inherited, along with its two or three blessings, the manifold curse of psychoanalysis: the assumption that the grounds of discontent, anger, rage, despair—

"unhappiness" in general—reside within the sufferer rather than outside of him. Psychoanalysis maintains that if the Oedipal aggressions of the male are a function merely of the domestic triangle, arising ineluctably out of the "family romance," so too are the female emotions—with the added embarrassment that the female is doomed to the greater imperfection of being both non-male and presumably resentful as a consequence of this condition. Aggression, discontent, rebellious urges, a sense of injustice—these have nothing to do with the outer world, but only with the sufferer; and if the sufferer is a woman, by definition a creature characterized by envy, how is it possible to take her seriously? The territory of the female artist should be the subjective, the domestic. She is allowed to be "charming," "amusing," "delightful." Her models should not be Shakespeare or Dostoyevsky but one or another woman writer. Her skills should be those of a conscientious seamstress.

"Why is your writing so violent?" Since it is commonly understood that serious writers, as distinct from entertainers or propagandists, take for their natural subjects the complexity of the world, its evils as well as its goods, it is always an insulting question; and it is always sexist.

The serious writer, after all, bears witness. The serious writer restructures "reality" in the service of his or her art, and surely hopes for a unique esthetic vision and some felicity of language; but reality is always the foundation, just as the alphabet, in whatever motley splendor, is the foundation of Finnegans Wake. (The claustrophobic nature of self-referential art is, perhaps, a paradigm of the infant's world: Nothing objective is grasped as real, everything refers inward, words appear to be created, enhanced with private meanings. Hence such an artist's contempt for "real" worlds and the sentimental hope for a forcible remaking of the universe—as if there were not a universe in existence beyond the artist's control.) So the serious male writer is allowed his vision and takes as his rightful subject a world as vast as Dostoyevsky's Russia, or Melville's oceans or Faulkner's "postage stamp of earth" in Mississippi. One does not inquire of them, "Why is your writing so violent?"

If the lot of womankind has not yet widely diverged from that romantically envisioned by our Moral Majority and by the late Adolf Hitler ("Kirche, Kinder, Kuchen"), the lot of the woman writer has been just as severely circumscribed. War, rape, murder and the more colorful minor crimes evidently fall within the exclusive province of the male writer, just as, generally, they fall within the exclusive province of male action.

Occasionally, however, a woman writer is told gravely, "You write like a man." Since this is the highest accolade, presented as a judgment from above and closed to any further discussion, it would be impolite to ask, "Which man? Any man? You?"

"Why is your writing so violent?" The question was asked in Liege, in Hamburg, in London, in Detroit, in New York City. It would be asked in China if I went to China. It would be asked in Moscow. In Hiroshima.

When I point out that, in fact, my writing isn't usually explicitly violent, but deals, most of the time, with the phenomenon of violence and its aftermath, in ways not unlike those of the Greek dramatists; when I point out that, in any case, writing is language and, in a very important sense, is more "about" language than "about" a subject — the interviewer will nod, and take notes, and inquire about my childhood: "Was it tragic? Have you been frightened by life?"

In recent years a variant has been added: How do I defend myself against "critical charges" that my writing is "violent"? How can I "justify" myself?

"Would you ask that question of a male writer," I responded, the last time it was put to me, not very long ago. After some hesitation, the answer came: "No." "Why not?" I asked. Herewith, a long pause ensued. My interrogator knew the answer to the question but declined to answer it. Or perhaps he was thinking. I hope he still is.

THE AMERICAN DREAM: A COURSE SYLLABUS

JOYCE CAROL OATES

Exploring the meaning of "The American Dream" through American literature and film.

Below is the syllabus for my course titled "The American Dream" which was my contribution to Princeton University's Freshman Seminar Program. In all, I taught this seminar twice, in spring terms 2020 and 2021; I would love to teach it again someday if my schedule allows. (Usually, at Princeton, I am teaching a fiction workshop in the Creative Writing Program.)

Seminars are limited to just ten students, by application only. Meetings are in seminar rooms in attractive buildings on campus but, unfortunately, our first semester was rudely (and permanently) interrupted when on March 11, 2020, the university shut down in the face of Covid, and our seminar moved to Zoom.

Students in "The American Dream" wrote numerous papers and kept journals; their final work was a project of some scope and ambition which was to be presented as a portfolio, a model of a small book with specially designed covers and, in some cases, illustrations. A typical weekly assignment might be to emulate the prose of, for instance, Thomas Jefferson in the *Declaration of Independence*, or Walt Whitman in *Leaves of Grass*; there is no better way to appreciate and comprehend great writers of the past than by studying their prose carefully and trying to reproduce it.

Each week students wrote critiques of the weekly assignment which was usually two thematically related texts for them to consider, like short stories by Mark Twain and Shirley Jackson on a similar theme.

Student projects were on a wide variety of subjects—politics, history, music, film, the immigrant experience (autobiographical), race relations, the endangered environment. One student wrote a memoir as the descendant of an enslaved Black woman and a white slaveholder in Virginia; another, of "gay themes" in the music and literature of the West. One paper was a detailed critique of images (stereotypes) of immigrants in Hollywood films; another, "The Chinese American Dream: Symbols and Subversions in Literature." A music major composed original music; another student, investigating "The Suburbs," created a journal so original and beautiful that it was a work of art which I showed visitors to my house for a week or two before returning it to him. Each student designed a book complete with original cover art and the traditional features of a trade book.

Yes, It was always something of a shock to be reminded that these exceptional students were freshmen…

In seminars, focus is on student participation, presentation of papers, and discussion. I have to say, without exaggeration, that my Freshman Seminar students were absolutely brilliant. Repeat: brilliant.

The last thing some of us did together, after the quarantine was lifted, was to attend Werner Herzog's presentation of his controversial film *Grizzly Man*, preceded by a communal dinner.

Dear Freshman Seminar students—

I am very much looking forward to meeting with you on Wed. Feb. 3, 1:30 p.m.—4:20 p.m. I will resend a Zoom invitation.

Enclosed is our syllabus for the spring term, which is slightly revised to include Amanda Gorman's inaugural poem (available online).

On Feb. 3 we will have an informal introductory class. seminars are all "informal"—participatory. seminars are not lectures or conventional classes but opportunities for students to participate in discussions. Both the quality of written work and seminar participation go into final grading.

For Feb. 3, you should be prepared to read from your personal journal (see syllabus) as well as to discuss *The Declaration of Independence* and the inaugural poems (Robert Frost's "The Gift Outright, Amanda Gorman's "The Hill We Climb"—both available online).

Readings are voluntary; you will not be called upon.

warmly, on a very snowy day—

—Joyce Carol Oates, Roger S. Berlind Professor of Humanities Emerita at Princeton University

THE AMERICAN DREAM: VISIONS & SUBVERSIONS
JOYCE CAROL OATES

- Text: *The Oxford Book of American Short Stories* (Second Edition, 2013), ed. Oates.
- *Song of Myself*, Walt Whitman
- *Born Yesterday* (film)
- *Blade Runner* (film)

Intention of course: to explore the meaning of "The American Dream" primarily through representative American short fiction.

Ideal? cliche? origin? how evolved? present time? future?

Each week brief papers (1–2 pp.) are due comparing and contrasting the stories assigned for that week and singling out representative passages of prose from each. These papers will be read aloud and discussed before being handed in to the instructor.

There will be a midterm paper (5–10 pp.) due in Week 6. (By Week 3 you should have informed me what your topic will be. See below for possible topics.) * Your independent topics—"special topics"—will be presented to the workshop. (30–45 minutes each).

A portfolio will be due at the end of the course, including these papers as well as a single longer paper (12–20 pp.) on a subject to be chosen. The grade for this portfolio will count for 40 percent of the course; shorter papers and seminar participation will each count for 30 percent.

You will be required to keep personal journals exploring the subject of the "American Dream." Each week you will be invited to read excerpts from your journals which can include cultural, social, political commentary in addition to personal experiences; reactions to recent events in American life; recommendations of films, art, music, books (whether new or old); advocacy in the public interest; "investigative" topics in timely or controversial subjects (journalism, creative non-fiction); interviews with relatives, immigrants, new Americans, minority citizens.

Suggestions for independent papers (midterm and final papers) include:

- Supplementary readings from the anthology: gender issues in Herman Melville, Charlotte Perkins Gilman; feminist issues in Nathaniel Hawthorne, Edith Wharton, Louise Erdrich; racial politics in Charles Chesnutt, Langston Hughes, Richard Wright and/or Eudora Welty; ecological/environmental issues in Sarah Orne Jewett; visions of "expatriate Americans" in Ernest Hemingway and Paul Bowles; materialism in Raymond Carver & T. C. Boyle; F. Scott Fitzgerald, and James Baldwin; "the male gaze"—William Carlos Williams, John Cheever, John Updike; minimalist techniques in Ernest Hemingway & Amy Hempel; humor/ irony in Donald Barthelme and Lorrie Moore
- Further readings in the poetry of Walt Whitman: *Leaves of Grass*
- Selected poems of Robert Frost, William Carlos Williams, Allen Ginsberg, Mary Oliver among others
- Edward Albee, *The American Dream*
- Arthur Miller, *Death of a Salesman*
- Tony Kushner, *Angels in America*
- August Wilson, selected plays
- Lorraine Hansberry, *A Raisin in the Sun*

- Suzan Lori-Parks, *The America Play*
- Emily Mann, *Still Life, Execution of Justice*
- Memoirs: Henry David Thoreau, James Baldwin, Malcolm X, Lorraine Hansberry, Edmund White, Annie Dillard, Tobias Wolff, Sherman Alexie, David Treuer (*Rez Life),* Mikal Gilmore, Mike Herr (*Dispatches),* Steve Martin (*Born Standing Up),* Mary Karr (*The Liars' Club),* David Sedaris, Tracy K. Smith, Jesmyn Ward
- Alexis de Tocqueville, *Democracy in America*
- Henry Adams, *The Education of Henry Adams*
- Films (*Born on the Fourth of July*, etc.), TV classic series (*Breaking Bad,* etc.), music (Springsteen, "Born in the USA," etc.), comedy (including 20th century & 21st century stand-up comics)
- American artists: Winslow Homer, Childe Hassam, Frederic Church,
- Thomas Cole, Albert Bierstadt, Martin Johnson Heade. Grandma Moses,
- Norman Rockwell, Andrew Wyeth
- Andy Warhol, Robert Rauschenberg, Jasper Johns, Claes Oldenburg.
- Walker Evans, Eudora Welty, Gary Winograd, Bruce Davidson, Diane Arbus, Niko J. Kallianiotis, Cindy Sherman, Jenny Holzer, Kiki Smith

Week 1. Introduction. "The Declaration of Independence"

Inaugural poems:

- Robert Frost, "The Gift Outright" (1961)
- Amanda Gorman, "The Hill We Climb" (2021)

Assignment for next week: Prose piece emulating Jefferson's language

Week 2: Washington Irving, "Rip van Winkle"

- Whitman (first seventeen sections of Whitman's *Song of Myself*)
- due: paragraph emulating Jefferson's prose style
- critique (1–2 pp.) of "Rip van Winkle"
- critique (1–2 pp.) of *Song of Myself*
- journal entry

Week 3: Stephen Crane, "The Little Regiment"

- Tim O'Brien, *The Things They Carried*
- *Song of Myself,* through section 33
- due: topics for mid-term papers
- critique of Crane and O'Brien stories
- emulation of a stanza of Whitman's poetry
- journal entry

Week 4: Jack London, Tobias Wolff

- final section, *Song of Myself*
- due: critique of London & Wolff stories
- critique of *Song of Myself*
- journal entry

Week 5: Samuel Clemens (Mark Twain), Shirley Jackson

- "visions of human nature"

- due: critique or creative response to Clemens, Jackson
- journal entry

Week 6: Comic vision: *Born Yesterday* (film, access Amazon Prime rental; Lorrie Moore

- midterm papers due
- presentation of special topics

Week 7: Jean Toomer, Ralph Ellison

- due: critique or creative response
- presentation of special topics

Week 8: William Faulkner, Flannery O'Connor

- due: topics for final papers
- critique or creative response
- presentation of special topics

Week 9: Annie Proulx, Pinckney Benedict

- due: critique or creative response
- presentation of special topics

Week 10: Bernard Malamud, Ha Jin

- due: critique of Malamud, Jin
- presentation of special topics

Week 11: Ray Bradbury, *Blade Runner* (film, Amazon Prime rental)

- due: critique or creative response
- presentation of special topics

Week 12: Jhumpa Lahiri, Junot Diaz

- due: critique of Lahiri, Diaz
- presentation of special topics

Portfolios due (date to come). Portfolios should contain all the work you have done for this semester as well as your long paper. You will be expected also to design a little book: front & back covers, table of contents, author photo & biography, "quotes" [you may use my comments on your work] and brief summary of contents.] We will discuss the portfolios in detail, so don't worry about this assignment beforehand.

THE PLUNGE

A STORY

JR MURRAY

Unlike the previous drivers they'd had since arriving on the island, this one kept to himself after a perfunctory greeting. Nothing to complain about, just not as effusive as the others, with their big smiles and barrage of friendly questions that punctuated their improvised scripts as each one assumed the role of self-appointed tour guide. Daniel was relieved right now, because it freed him from feeling obliged to make chitchat in an effort not to seem like some rich American tourist who didn't respect the natives. He could just sit in silence and watch the scenery as the van bumped along the narrow roadway, the ocean to the right, jungle-covered hills to the left. A few miles past the resort, the oceanfront charm dissipated with the roadside trash and corrugated tin structures that looked to be abandoned or on the verge of collapsing. Occasionally, one might be occupied by a random little business like a car mechanic's shop, a dry goods market, or a tackle store, but none of them seemed to have any customers.

The drive made Daniel think of his family's summer sojourns to their cottage on Cape Cod. His parents were in the front seat, kids in the back, spying an occasional glimpse of ocean but more often looking at all the roadside businesses that reflected the culture of seashore towns—lobster roll stands, sail repair services, ice cream shops, seashell stores, and the occasional Irish pub. It was only about 150 miles from home but seemed like another world to someone who'd only been out of New England twice on family vacations to New York and Montreal, neither of which he could clearly remember. Even their cottage had a totally different look from their Connecticut house. A fraction of the size, with bleached wood shingles instead of white-painted clapboard, it had a lobster pot coffee table in the center of the living room, captain's chairs around the kitchen table, and a reproduction of Winslow Homer's "The Fog Warning" hanging above the couch. By the standards of his life now, the place was a cramped, mildew-infested shack, but back then, he felt that his family was on par with the Kennedys.

"Dammit," he muttered, still looking out the front window of the van in an attempt to avoid the motion sickness he was so prone to.

"What?" Anna wasn't especially interested, just obliged to ask.

"I forgot sunscreen. I'll get totally burned."

"Right here." She reached into her raffia tote, pulled out a drawstring sack, and showed him three choices of sunscreen. "Relax."

"Perfectly relaxed. I just don't want to spend the rest of the vacation sprawled out on a bed in agony, like in Kauai."

The idea of sunburn made him think of Leila, who had his fair skin but who resented his reminders to reapply sunscreen and warnings that she'd pay the price decades from now for careless sun exposure. Chase was more like his wife, totally bronzed after two days in the sun. A brief flash of his own summers on the Cape with a permanently sunburned nose, despite the zinc oxide and wide-brimmed hats, convinced Daniel that a boy who could get a proper tan was at an advantage in all aspects of life.

He quickly glanced at them in the seat behind him.

"Really, you two? Phones?" Seeming to be on the verge of exasperation despite the fact that he rarely interrupted them, each of them pulled out one earbud to hear him. "Every teenager on the planet can be looking at Instagram right now; you guys get to look at this other *world*."

"I've *been* looking, I picked up my phone right before you turned around!" Then, to herself, "Ugh..."

His son replaced his earbud and remained silent, but Daniel knew he was probably glaring at the back of his head in full irritation mode.

Anna was deleting emails from her phone, her nail audibly clicking on the screen. "There's really nothing so special they need to look at right now," remarked Anna.

"It's another aesthetic, another climate, another culture—another way of living. It's worth seeing. Better than consumption-obsessed, self-absorbed social media posts worshipping fame and fortune. And better than the radiation exposure they're probably getting," replied Daniel.

"Tell them that. That'll really convince them."

He leaned forward when he realized they were nearing another village as they hit the speed bumps in the road. "Look," he told her, "another one."

She glanced up momentarily, replacing her iPhone in her bag and pulling out a nail file.

"Don't you just love it? All this communal living? People looking out for each other, treating each other as equals, making sure everyone has enough..." He trailed off as he realized once again that he was the only one enthused by the whole thing.

"*Is* it so great? Aren't they basically poor and living in squalor?" She was intently focused on the corner of the nail on her ring finger. "A lot of those places don't have windows or doors. I think it's just...sad."

"Well, it's sad if you think that what you have isn't enough, but they seem pretty happy to me. And by the way, have you seen any affluent neighborhoods since we got here?"

"They're probably all hidden behind gates like everywhere else." She glanced down at his chin, "What's that? I like a man with a cleft chin, but what's going on *there*?"

"From shaving." He wet his fingertip on his tongue and tried to rub off the dried blood.

The van turned off the road onto a driveway pocked with deep puddles. They passed a rugby field and a junkyard of tires before pulling up to a tidy, corrugated tin structure painted bright yellow, with two shiny red picnic tables and a Pepsi vending machine in front of it. In the gravel lot beside it was a conga line of dune buggies.

"This is it, mistah." The driver's first words since they passed the gatehouse of the resort.

Two men wearing uniforms of red shorts and yellow T-shirts exited the building to greet them. One, with straight black hair and a big belly, was obviously in charge. The other, younger one had a closely cut afro, an athlete's body, and an air of someone who had more influence than he got credit for. By the way they comported themselves, Daniel's first impression was that, since he was standing back a bit, holding a clipboard, and looking serious, the big guy's father owned the business. But he thought that its survival depended on the fit guy, whose smile and swaggering confidence made you trust him to guide you into remote jungle.

The two of them greeted everyone with a "Bula!" The fit guy, Ratu, seemed more genuine, with his broad smile of perfect teeth and lingering eye contact. Although he had an obvious underbite, he had a handsome face with a square jaw, and large, wide-set, amber eyes.

Anna responded with an enthusiastic "Bula!" as she stepped out of the van. Daniel smiled as he walked toward them and offered his hand. They could make a charming first impression when they felt like it.

After the greeting, their hosts brought them to the picnic table where the serious guy, Nick, had them fill out paperwork while Ratu fitted each of them for helmets. Leila sniffed the padding lining the helmet and bobbed her head backward with a scowl before turning to her brother, Chase, and mouthing, "Smell it." He did and looked back to her before saying "Gross" in reply.

Daniel, watching the exchange, said, "There's no option, you guys, so..." They put their helmets on with a combination of resignation and disgust.

The men escorted them down to their buggies and got them situated, parents in one, kids in the other. The guides got into an enclosed jeep to lead the way. As they passed the rugby field, they hit their first puddle, deeper than it looked, which doused them with muddy water. They all laughed incredulously.

"Oh, my God," Daniel said to Anna through his helmet, "what are we paying for this abuse?" They both laughed.

"You don't want to know, but it's worth it!"

At that moment, he was genuinely enjoying himself, but there was always a side of him that just wanted to be reading his book, lying in the hammock on the beach in front of their villa. His work was stressful, and his blood pressure was high; in his mind, vacations were for decompressing.

Although they could easily afford it, it sometimes bothered him that they spent so much money doing extra activities on vacations. Guided hikes to waterfalls, private boat rides to islands, spearfishing lessons, scuba diving lessons, cooking lessons—their travel agent could arrange anything they wanted. Using income from her trust, Anna planned not just a vacation but an "experience" every summer. The resorts they stayed at were too exclusive to be crowded, so the pools and the beaches were always beautiful and sparsely populated. We shouldn't need anything more, he often thought to himself. His parents had never scheduled any extra outings for their beach vacations—sand, ocean, and long summer days were all they needed to be happy.

After a couple of minutes, the cracked, pot-holed pavement turned into loose gravel and then a dirt path. Their buggies' engines were loud, exhaust emitting, and seemingly no more powerful than lawnmowers. After a forty-minute ride into the jungle, winding up and down steep hills on a six-foot-wide path where they occasionally lost traction in muddy stretches or got slapped by leaves leaning into their path, their guides pulled into a small clearing halfway up a hill, hopped out, and instructed them to do the same.

"Now we hike," said Nick, nodding to the entrance of an unmarked path that descended into the lush green jungle. The four of them got out of their buggies in a much lighter mood than they'd gotten into them, competing for who'd gotten the wettest or the muddiest and whose buggy was harder to drive.

Ratu leaned into the back of the SUV, transferring packages and bottles from a cooler to duffle bags. He turned around to face them with a big smile. "Now, family! You ready for adventure?"

"Let's do it!" said Anna.

Nick grabbed a duffle from the SUV, and they followed him to begin the trek down the hill to the waterfall with Ratu at the back, wearing a backpack and carrying another, larger duffle.

The muddy trail proved challenging at its steepest spots. At some point each of them had to grab hold of one of the bamboo trees lining the path to reestablish their balance as they slipped and slid their way down the leafy, narrow trail, dappled with sunlight. They heard running water as the hill began to level off, and a stream came into view that ultimately ran parallel with the trail.

"Wow, you guys see the stream?" Daniel knew he was asking an obvious question, but he was trying to maintain the enthusiasm they'd had when they got out of their buggies.

"Yeah, nice," his daughter called back.

"Did you notice the way that the…" At that moment, not realizing that as the path had flattened out, so had the depth of the muddy sections, Daniel felt his right foot slide out in front of him on a 45-degree angle, forcing him to do a split. First his left knee, then his right elbow, then the right side of his body, and then the right side of his face hit the mud. He wasn't out of shape, he worked out every morning at six, but he wasn't used to exercising outside of a gym.

"Shit!"

The guides were immediately on him, pulling him up and checking to see if he was injured, or angry, or anything else that might result in a bad review of their little business.

"I'm fine, I'm fine. Do you have something I can wipe my face with?" Nick pulled a hand towel from his duffle and held it out for Daniel, but Ratu intercepted it and, still wearing his backpack and carrying his duffle, went to the stream to douse it.

Daniel glanced over at his family, who were doing all they could to contain their laughter. "Really? You're laughing?" He was trying to sound good-natured, as if he thought it was kind of funny, too, even though he thought his elbow and knee might be bleeding.

"I'm sorry. Are you okay?" Anna offered a patronizing look of concern that only fueled his humiliation.

"I'm fine…my…nothing. I'm fine."

That served as a cue for his children to release their pent-up laughter. He looked at them with a wounded expression.

"I'm sorry, Dad," Leila said, "it's just that your face…and your hair is standing up on that side."

Ratu came up next to him with the wet towel. "You okay, Dad? No injuries?"

"No injuries, I think." He reached for the towel, but Ratu pulled it away.

"I got it, Dad." Ratu gently wiped the mud from Daniel's face with an expertise that made it seem that it was a routine service performed for all his customers, and which should have mitigated the humiliation of falling, but which embarrassed him a little further. "We are almost there—and then you jump in the water and be like new." Ratu flashed his big, contagious grin, and they moved on.

They heard the waterfall well in advance of seeing it, and the guides stepped in front of them to offer a hand to help them over the slippery rocks abutting the pool. It was then that Daniel noticed Ratu's feet.

"Wait, you're barefoot! Have you been barefoot the whole time?"

The whole family looked down at Ratu's muddy feet incredulously.

"Not barefoot, Dad. Fijian shoes!" They all chuckled before moving in an almost enchanted state toward a turquoise pool fed by a fifty-foot waterfall bordering a third of its circumference. High up, at the crest of the waterfall, the water glowed with bright sunlight.

Daniel sat down on a boulder and untied his mud-covered hiking shoes. The guides and Anna joined him.

"Well," Anna said, "I guess those fancy hiking shoes couldn't compete with a pair of Fijian shoes." The guides and Anna smiled at her joke as Daniel tried to concentrate on undoing the double knot he'd tied in his laces that morning.

"Funny stuff, Anna. Thanks."

"What do you mean, 'thanks'?"

"Nothing."

"Okay, family!" Ratu clapped his hands. "Time for swimming!"

Leila and Chase walked to the edge of the water.

As the two guides watched them, Daniel decided that his daughter had outgrown her bikini, even though he'd never seen it before. It then occurred to him that the guides were in complete control over him and his family.

"Can I go in?" His son always had to be the first one in the water.

"Absolutely!" Anna called out as she walked toward the pool. She was wearing what she called (since it offered more coverage than her daughter's) her "lady's bikini," not looking, Daniel thought, like a middle-aged woman who'd carried two children to term.

The teens both jumped in, followed by Anna. Daniel began inspecting his elbow, which had evidently hit something more than soft mud when he fell, since it was swollen and bleeding. Ratu walked past him shirtless, his shorts hanging low on his hips.

"Come on, Dad!"

Nick kept his clothes on and began to go through the duffle bags and cooler, spreading out a tablecloth on a weathered bamboo table that past tour guides had stashed next to the trail. He set up a luncheon of cold cuts, potato chips, dill pickles, papaya slices, and celery sticks.

Daniel walked very gingerly toward the water, his rarely bare feet sensitive to every lump and edge on the rocks. He found a large, flat rock about a foot below the surface at the water's edge. He stood on it, grateful for the cool relief on his feet as he watched his children scaling a boulder next to the waterfall and his wife doing a backstroke across the center of the pool. Then he noticed Ratu on all fours, climbing the rocks up to the base of the waterfall. When he got there, he stood on a large rock under the curtain of falling water, face up, smiling as usual, arms stretched out in front of him like a beckoning holy man.

Daniel studied him with a combination of irritation and envy as he considered his youth, his confidence, his fearlessness. Daniel felt he'd spent his own life constantly jumping through hoops to prove some aspect of his own legitimacy, but here at a waterfall in the jungle, none of that mattered. Here, Ratu was the man to envy.

Leila and Chase had jumped from their boulder into the pool and were now heading toward Ratu. Daniel sat on his flat rock, which left him submerged to the hips, allowing him to wash off the mud. He watched as his children disappeared behind the waterfall, only to reemerge under the curtain of water about five feet above where they'd entered. That's when he noticed that Ratu was rock climbing diagonally up the wall and away from the curtain of water until he reached a small shelf, no more than a foot deep, thirty feet above the pool. He carefully positioned himself facing out, his back to the rock.

"Okay, family, here I go!" Careful to avoid the rocks bordering the pool below, he launched himself from the ledge and did a slow cycling action with his feet, arms stretched out above him like an Olympian crossing the finish line. Anna and the kids paused their own activities to watch his jump and then clapped and whooped enthusiastically.

Anna was now climbing the rocks at the base of the waterfall, in the direction of her children. Ratu came out of the pool behind her. The falling water blocked out their voices, but Daniel could see Ratu call to Anna and Anna turn around and smile at him. A few seconds later, the four of them met up on a wide ledge just left of the curtain of water. Led by Ratu, they all joined hands and jumped, making an enormous splash on impact, and then each bobbing to the surface and smiling.

"Dad," his daughter called out, "come in!"

He gave her a "thumbs up" followed by a "just a minute" signal. He was hot and he was dirty. He knew the water would feel good, but he felt a knot in his throat—maybe anger, maybe sadness, maybe resignation to the loneliness he too often felt when he shouldn't feel lonely, when he was with his family (and away from his work).

Anna and Ratu again climbed out of the pool and scaled the rock wall, Ratu leading her higher than they'd gone with Leila and Chase. As he ascended to each new ledge, he'd turn back and hold his hand out to Anna, who grabbed it and joined him on small rock shelves, often shoulder to shoulder if not hip to hip, until they arrived at a wide swath of rock that was tucked into the hillside, further away from the waterfall. She had a history of chumming up to younger men they'd hired. The Pilates instructor, the landscape architect, the guitar teacher, the head of development at the museum—Daniel thought she too often entered their personal space, touched them unnecessarily. He suspected that she'd cheated on him, and her best friend's husband had intimated as much after too many scotch and sodas, but Daniel never sought confirmation. Dreading it was easier than confirming it.

Daniel then realized that they were heading toward a rope swing that someone had tied onto the thick branch of an enormous dakua tree growing near the edge of the pool. From there, someone could grab hold of the rope and get a running start before launching from the edge, swinging toward the center, and dropping into the turquoise water far below.

Daniel studied Ratu, who was holding the rope, walking back and forth, looking over the edge and down to the water. Then he studied Anna and how she chattered and gestured and smiled at Ratu, seemingly in awe of his considering the jump. As Ratu backed up to prepare for his jump, Anna stood back, fists clenched together and pressed against her breastbone, looking like an awestruck teenage fan.

"Oh, give me a break, Anna," Daniel mumbled to himself. He didn't mind her snarkiness with him, but he couldn't abide the flirting. He took his shirt off and jumped into the water, simultaneously treading water and washing off the remaining mud from his fall.

"Dad," his daughter called out, "look!" She gestured up to Ratu, who was holding onto the rope with an uncharacteristically serious expression as he launched over the water. When he was perfectly centered above the pool, he flashed his broad smile before letting go and entering the water with barely a splash. Anna bounced on the balls of her feet, clapping wildly and woo-hooing so loudly that it echoed all around them.

Daniel swam across the pool toward the waterfall, forgetting the bumps and scrapes he'd incurred when he fell. He felt strong and purposeful and proudly masculine. He'd never been much of an athlete, but his regular workouts kept him in good shape, and he possessed a degree of physical confidence when he didn't think too much about it.

He climbed up through the curtain of the waterfall and began scaling the rock to reach the plateau where Anna stood. He didn't notice that Ratu was ten feet behind him, sometimes having to pause, since Daniel climbed at a slower pace.

When Daniel finally reached Anna, she turned around and smiled, but the first thing out of his mouth was, "It would be nice if you could act like you're a married woman with two teenagers watching you."

Anna stared at him coldly, all the happy expression gone from her face. He still felt his anger, but her resistance was making him question himself. He wanted to say something sharp and penetrating, but all he could manage was, "You know? Okay?" In five seconds, he'd segued from admonishing to almost pleading.

"*You* have a problem," she said dismissively. Just then, Ratu joined them.

"All right, Dad! You made it!"

Daniel couldn't muster up any charm for Ratu. "Yeah, Ratu, I made it. Show me how I do this rope swing. I need to get back in the water."

"Oh, Mister Daniel, I think maybe you don't want to do that."

"Daniel," Anna said, "don't be ridiculous."

"I'm not being ridiculous." He walked over to the edge, looked down at his kids, and clapped his hands, causing them to look up. He pointed to himself and then to the rope. They both watched him intently, his son smiling, his daughter slack jawed. He held the rope with all his might, backed up as far as the rope allowed, and stared at the edge.

"Mr. Daniel, please don't. It's very dangerous. I could get in trouble."

"I'm just jumping in the water. You won't get in any trouble."

Vibrating with an unleashed anger that somehow felt exhilarating, he bolted to the edge and leapt into the air. As the rope neared its full extension over the water, his anger transformed into fearlessness and then, as he quickly glanced at Anna and Ratu and then his children, into pure joy. With that lightness, his grip loosened prematurely, and he slid five feet down the slack of rope before regaining his grip, at which point he realized he'd missed his opportunity to drop into the turquoise center of the pool and was now swinging back toward the rock wall, five feet beneath the point where he'd launched, with nowhere to jump off and nothing but rocks below.

THREE POEMS

RALPH J. LONG, JR.

Dermatology

It doesn't matter that you rode every subway line
or one Saturday you lost your last twenty dollars
to a carny at the Feast of San Gennaro and walked
home over the Brooklyn Bridge in cheap espadrilles
leaving you with blisters almost as bad as those after
a Hampton's weekend trip where beer failed to provide
immunity to sunburn with even the soles of your feet
throbbing with pain equaling the dermatologist's nitrous
oxide spray that you will experience four decades later
when peeling skin may or may not be a sign of healing
as you slowly realize most of your new acquaintances
are medical professionals and tradespeople whose fees
grow exponentially with each question and consultation.

Enough

It doesn't matter that Honey Baked was sold out
on the day before Easter because the Bay Bridge
maze is moving at the speed limit and the clouds
over Oakland would have pleased Ansel Adams
and you are inhaling the wafting aroma of slowly
cooling baby back ribs in the back seat that will
carry over to the kitchen when they are reheated
in a low oven while you search for paper napkins
to mop up the sauce that you don't need because
the pit master was a BBQ savant and weeks after
you suck the bones clean, you will savor this day.

Thinking about Home on the 4th of July

An ordinary block just long enough that
hair wet from the shower froze in winter
and summer seersucker wilted before the
sanctuary of the subway tunnel at its end.
A blue-collar hodgepodge-stucco, brick
and shingle; stoops resounded with Italian
and Polish, not the Ireland-rooted majority's
lost Gaelic. All were Americans on the 4th.
Old flags dragged from closets hung limp
in the rising heat, the scent of lighter fluid
signaled charred hot dogs and hamburgers.
Children waited for the firework lightning
smuggled from New Jersey. The street's vets
were divided. The untried drank beer and lied,
while the silent hoped to forget, draining cups
fortified by spirits of lands that haunted them.
One held to an annual mission as dangerous as
any the Army had required. Provisioned with
two bottles of whisky, he left his house fleeing
memory before the firecrackers and M-80's
returned the jungle and mortars and napalm.
If he was lucky he fell into his own bed, if not,
his wife feared the night as if he was deployed.
Neighbors judged his drinking, ignoring who
he was the other three hundred sixty-four days.

WHAT ABOUT WRITERS?!

AN ESSAY

MICHAEL ROSS

New Literary Project encourages a variety of writers in several meaningful and successful ways. It offers the Joyce Carol Oates Prize of $50,000 to mid-career authors of fiction and $5,000 summer awards to creative writers who teach high school across the US. Perhaps most important, NewLit collaborates to offer fellowships to creative writing teachers from the University of California, Berkeley (Bonnie Bonetti-Bell Fellows) and from Saint Mary's College of California (Iris Starn Fellows). In 2024 these fellows conducted nine writing workshops at sites such as Girls Inc. Alameda County, Contra Costa County Juvenile Hall, and elsewhere, in public schools and after-school programs.

One of my most recent volumes of quotations collected from my reading of literary fiction, *Ross's Literary Discoveries,* includes numerous quotes about writers. Some are somewhat negative, while others explain how difficult writers' tasks and lives are. Others are simply descriptive, and others offer accolades and expressions of appreciation for authors. Here are some examples from my book.

We start with a non-judgmental observation about why writers write:

But after all every writer writes because it's his mode of living.

F. SCOTT FITZGERALD, *The Beautiful and Damned*

This quote casts an aspersion on writers without any explanation or apparent justification:

What lunatics writers are...

ELIZABETH GOUDGE, *The Scent of Water*

This is a somewhat frequent complaint about writers' supposed lack of sufficient life experience:

Writing is one thing, but experiencing life is more important.

CRISTINA HENRIQUEZ,
"Mercury" in *Come Together, Fall Apart*

I suppose that because writing is usually a solitary endeavor, it allows for a fair dose of mischief:

He was a writer. A writer. They have time to get into trouble.

MICHAEL ONDAATJE, *Anil's Ghost*

Here is a somewhat ironic observation about the relationship between the writer and his or her reader:

...the writer wrote alone, and the reader read alone, and they were alone together.

S. BYATT, *Possession*

I cannot verify that Thoreau said this, but I like the humor in any case:

Thoreau said a writer was a man with nothing to do who finds something to do.

RICHARD FORD, *The Lay of the Land*

I wonder if many writers would agree with this ironic quote:

...certainly a life of writing books is a trying adventure in which you cannot find out where you are unless you lose your way.

PHILIP ROTH, *The Counterlife*

I like this picturesque simile for novelists' uncertainty about success:

Writing novels is like putting messages into bottle after bottle and tossing them into the sea on the outgoing tide without any idea of where they'll be washed up or how they will be interpreted.

DAVID LODGE, *Home Truths*

The simile in this quote makes the author's point quite vividly and efficiently:

"The fact that a writer needed solitude didn't mean he was cut off or selfish. A writer was like a monk in his cell praying for the world—something he performed alone, but for other people." *

TOBIAS WOLFF, *Old School*

Here is a depiction of how challenging the nature of the novelist's work can be:

I played a mild hunch. That's what writing is, a hundred hunches, a hundred affronts to your confidence, a hundred decisions, every page.

MARTIN AMIS, *London Fields*

This quote uses a very descriptive metaphor of a sensory experience to describe what it is like for the author to begin his or her novel:

Starting a novel is opening a door on a misty landscape; you can still see very little, but you can smell the earth and feel the wind blowing.

IRIS MURDOCH, *Under the Net*

This seems like very good advice, but I suspect many writers hope to accomplish more than the duty ascribed here:

A writer cannot change the world; his duty is to describe it.

JOHN HERSEY, *The Conspiracy*

It is obvious that we do not judge writers' works by watching how they write, unlike how we assess the quality of some performances by watching the performer:

The skill of writing offers little to a viewer.

MICHAEL ONDAATJE, *Divisadero*

Is this the simple recipe for writers' success, and, if it is, how easy is it to follow?:

"It was the whole point of being a writer, wasn't it, to embrace the stuff of life? It was the whole point of life to embrace it." *

GRAHAM SWIFT, *Mothering Sunday*

Here is a clarion call for writers to write!:

*"Why not write, then... There is music in words, and it can be heard, you know, by thinking."**

E. L. DOCTOROW, *Homer & Langley*

Writing, in whatever genre, novels, short stories, poetry or nonfiction, deserves attention and encouragement. Writing requires the exercise of imagination, perseverance and critical judgment. Helping young people to write whatever moves them to do so, and rewarding talented creative writers wherever they are, enriches not only the writers but also their readers and all of society.

**Quoting a character speaking in, or the narrator of, the book referenced.*

POEM

HEATHER TONE

The Palace

This memo arrives from Palace. This monogrammed linen
    from his pocket, which he throws
        toward the crowd as an act of charity.
He is larger than the largest cloud. He is his utmost
    completion. You can bandy about
        details. You can make a point. You can draw
lines from point to point to make a cathedral.
    Palace cares not.
        In the palace, supper is served late after several cocktails
and a game of chance and missile.
    In the palace, every corner hides a nesting eagle.
        Palace, the eagles hiss as intrigues sift through their wings.
All my lovers: come back to the palace!
    Palace, she says into the phone, and she sounds like
        she wants me to pay for the dial.

Palace drifts through my sleep life like
    Abercrombie and Fitch. Those decorated boys
        strapped to pink chairs, then tilting
their chins for a profile. My stars, it is the Sun
    King! He nods his great cotton head and nearly topples.
        He's my favorite king, the King of Palaces.
I, too, would like to be called something
    associated with a celestial body. My middle name
        is *Whisper Well*, my daughter's *Avenue-*

by-the-Sea. In the pool is a blue palace swimmers break
with sharp elbows. I wanted to wear one on my back, like I was
born a god, my palace, a floating piece of light.

I woke myself this morning and entered door number one.
Someone called it "daylight," but I called it
"door number one," one of several thresholds
I had to cross, and with my eyes closed, I crossed it.
This is one of the beautiful things
about games in the palace—you can, must, be
half-asleep to play them. As an example, *palace me*
and you have won. My heart
gets fat in the trees. My heart blows up the woods
in the end. The woods at the edge of the palace
grounds are brittle compared to spells I speak
from the palace wall, to end palace walls.

Is this a movie? The palace is gray, no,
white, no, the color of gelatin. The palace
has pale steps from knees to throat.
Everyone is on set, set to break
hearts and let gauze from costumes blow
backward: holy show, cloven blow.
The audience looks a little concerned.
Well, they should be. This is a bad Palace: it rises
and rises like a terrible campfire.

WHIRLING

A STORY

H. L. ONSTAD

Devon wore the boat hat—blue with Saint Augustine's school insignia, two white oars crossed on an embroidered field of gold. Despite the ranger's booming voice, Devon had trouble making out the words over the heads of his classmates. He couldn't see the ranger's lips, hear his intonations. He turned away and watched a bird land, skitter across the path, and disappear over the ledge.

Father Leahy scanned the class, he believed the class's comportment to be a measure of his esteem. Devon's mother Rita was watching too, a peripheral set of eyes. Devon's arms were draped over his knees. He was in his own world. When he spoke, his speech often suffered from elision, syllables eclipsed, cut off, left behind. Devon reached for a rock in the sand, grazing the spindly arm of a cactus.

"Don't touch that," Rita said. Her face was sharp and he drew his hand back. Rita remembered when Devon's father had stepped on a cholla cactus off-trail, his toes coated in needles, the spines hooking ever deeper into his flesh, under the nails, into the soft ankle skin. The spines can leap toward prey, be mistaken for blades of grass, and embed their fine, barbed, hair-like glochids anywhere—they can even catch in your throat.

The ranger talked about the stratigraphy of the flat layers, the tectonic upheaval, a collision which occurred 1.7 billion years ago, the break up of a supercontinent. Devon was watching a kettle of turkey vultures riding a thermal wave. Rita inhaled audibly. They'd come all this way.

"You wanna get closer up, so you can listen?" She stood and reached for his hand, but he resisted. She turned to take in the vast layered rock before her, millions of years of compression. She glanced back at her boy, he pretended he didn't see her watching him. Not hearing well left him in a small darkened room of his own, where he could go to be alone—where he only faintly heard the world, as if it were mumbling prayers around him.

The sun scolded them for being where they don't belong, in the desert heat. Devon was sitting on the rock wall near the path with the rest of his class while the ranger spoke, then he leaned closer to his mother, Rita. She unscrewed the top of her water bottle and handed it to him. He took a sip and leaned forward.

"The story is in the rocks," the ranger said. Veined schists. 650 million years ago. The Great Unconformity. The ranger's words hummed, dipped, and rose. Devon felt their faint vibrations at a distance—their meaning lost. At school, Devon squirreled away unnoticed. Small for his age, and with the hearing loss, making friends required extra work, which he wasn't always willing to do. His father had left the family when he was five. Devon had stopped asking when his father would return. Friends had told Rita she was better off, Rita always nodded along, but secretly she believed her ex would return one day. She hadn't seen Richard for almost three years. Still she was *Mrs.* and wore the ring.

The tour ended just before 3pm. Students fanned out, already on the path back to the hotel. Devon sat up, turned to Rita.

"Let's go down the trail," he said. "Please."

"You're not drinking enough water." She handed him the water bottle.

He spun the cap and took a long sip and handed it back. She stowed it in her backpack. They hadn't fully explored the rim yet, but the day had been long and hot and Rita needed something less challenging.

"Let's check out the gift shop," she said. They walked in the languorous heat. Devon took off his hat to let the sweat escape.

"Mom,"

"What?"

"Just a little ways," he said and pointed to the dirt path that led into the canyon. "I just want to see it. " He took a few steps from her.

"No. C'mon, Devon. It's dangerous," she said and pulled him back. "We'll look into it tomorrow. I have to work up to it. I can't even stand near the edge." From the moment they arrived Rita felt unnerved by the depth of the canyon, the way emptiness was its own space. It was a feeling she hadn't expected.

"I'll be careful, I promise."

"No!"

Devon's face crinkled, as he walked beside her.

The gift shop was an island of cool, attached to a traditional Hopi house, long shelves stacked with woven rugs, reed and willow baskets, dreamcatchers dangling. Devon moved toward the kachina dolls, carefully arranged, and observed them until he identified what made each one unique—round yellow eyes and birdlike wings, a green skirt with a foxtail, boots with pink tassels, twigs of spruce in the left hand. Devon knew they would be too expensive. His eyes blinked quickly, tracing possibilities.

He spun a postcard rack. Glossy sunsets, striated rock, the lodge at Phantom Ranch, an aerial photo, native dwellings. He picked that last one.

Outside the Hopi house, a crowd had formed. Devon saw a girl his own age in a yellow t-shirt, her dark hair hung from under a straw brim. She sat next to a singer on the far side of the square. A flute sounded. The singer called. A drum beat. A man in traditional dress emerged, his body bent low to the ground, stepping with high knees. He exploded upright in a twirl of fringe and skipped across the ground hopping from foot to foot. Devon felt a jolt pulse through him. He listened to the rise and fall of the singer's voice, in time with the drum. He moved closer to get a better view, watching the man's body move, bounce, feathers and beads in flight. Rita sat on a bench nearby, as Devon moved deeper into the crowd. New performers entered, oscillating into a mirror world. He looked for details in their costumes, no two the same. He felt the beat of the drum in his chest, his waking self riveted, but another self began to slip away with the sounding bells, the whirling, the fringe rising as the dancers spun, so alive in the heat. They occupied an absence he felt within. Parallel to this world was another, he sensed. He wanted to fuse with it. Pure energy darted across the ground, moving into his limbs, no longer his own.

When it ended, the dancers left the square. Devon and Rita reunited and turned to head back to their hotel room. The sun was lower now, the sky haunted by a dying sun.

"Cool, huh?" she said. Devon didn't know if she was talking about the muted colors in the sky or the dancers. He nodded, and looked back to see people emptying out, returning to whatever they'd been doing before, same as ever.

"Will we come back?" he asked.

"I have to check the itinerary."

Rita was looking forward to getting back to the room with some time to relax before dinner. They reached their hotel in minutes and she rummaged in her bag for the key.

"I'm going to take a bath," she said.

Later that evening, the air still thick with heat, a tall ranger approached Father Leahy and asked him what he remembered about the afternoon and whether he noticed anything unusual about Devon earlier in the day. The ranger watched Father Leahy carefully.

"You know, the class, it's a large group. I have to keep track of them all. My attention is often divided." Father Leahy wiped his forehead with a white handkerchief. He pursed his lips, hunting for his words. "I know, he was there, with the group, his mother, of course. She keeps a close watch on him."

"Did Devon say anything to you?"

"No. No, I don't think so," he said. "He's a quiet kid, some hearing loss, an accident I'm told." In truth, Father Leahy had never bothered much with Devon. The boy was nearly deaf and it affected his performance in school; Father Leahy had discounted him.

"What about Mrs. Maldonado, did you talk with her today?"

"Rita was with the group most of the time. No, I didn't speak with her directly." The ranger scribbled in his notebook, small lined paper. Father Leahy peered downward and took the handkerchief from his pocket and dabbed his forehead again. He felt the Arizona heat under his long, dark robe.

"Do you think he headed down the trail alone?"

"From what I gather, he showed an interest in that," Father Leahy paused, then stiffened. "Boy needs discipline. Seems impulsive. Off on his own, no guide, no preparation, no backpack. *Fools rush in…*" Father Leahy stopped himself. He knew better than to say too much. The ranger touched the brim of his Stetson and tugged it down, meeting his eyes.

"You're sure you didn't see anything unusual?"

Father Leahy cleared his throat. In Albuquerque, long ago, there had been an accusation. Nothing was proven, it was raised and dropped. He'd been reassigned before anything further developed, transferred to a small parish in Flagstaff. A quiet place. He liked Flagstaff. He'd been able to put the whole thing behind him. Two years ago, he'd been reassigned again to Saint Augustine's. But, he'd never forget the humiliation of that initial episode. Now, he knew better. Had learned circumspection. To pass judgment was unpopular. Always trouble. Much had changed since he'd been in school, enduring his own father's discipline.

"I didn't see anything unusual," he said. The ranger thanked him and scanned the area near the rim, his eyes locked on Rita, who was being coaxed by another chaperone to come sit and rest. More rangers had arrived, expanding the cordoned area.

"Mrs. Maldonado," a ranger called to her. He waved her over.

Rita hurried towards him.

"News?" Her eyes pleaded.

"Not yet. I just want to be sure there isn't anything else you can think of, that might help us. Is anything missing?" Rita shook her head.

"No," she shook her head. "He's not the type to wander. He's never done that." The ranger nodded.

"But he asked about going down the trail?"

"Yes. Several times, he brought it up. Said he just wanted to see it. I told him it was dangerous. We were by the gift shop. We watched the dancers…" she shook her head, felt warmth flush her cheeks, her eyes burning, blurring.

"OK," he said. "Why don't you two wait together. I'll keep you updated."

Rita needed to pace. She walked back and forth inching closer to the rim, fidgeting with her hands, her ring. The gentle colors of the sky mocked her alarm. *Where is he?* The search team combed the area. The helicopter menaced the air as dusk settled. Darkness came, a triangular glow of light at the edges of the canyon illuminated brush and dust from the trail, but they found no trace of the boy.

Rita and Father Leahy waited inside. They had never had much to say to one another, even when Rita worked at the chapel, cleaning.

"They know what they're doing. I'm sure they'll find him," Father said. Rita barely lifted her eyes. Father Leahy blinked quickly. He ventured further. "In times like these, let the Lord be a comfort."

Rita scanned the ground. *Let the Lord be a comfort.* The sound of Father's voice jarred something inside of her and she recalled an incident in the chapel, when she had just started working there. He had been there. *Let the Lord be a comfort.* He was partially obscured by a formidable pillar. It was a glimpse, she knew, perhaps she was wrong, and couldn't imagine what it might mean for her to be right, so she'd never spoken of it to anyone. But now, she felt sure.

"Shut up," she said.

His mother's bathwater was running. The made beds, the icy air in the room were not welcoming. Rita had brought books from the library for him to read. Devon went to look, *Tewa Tales of Suspense!* He leafed a few pages then moved to the window, pulling back the heavy curtain with the plastic rod. The rim was right there. Tufts of white clouds gave way to peach streaks in the sky. Devon wanted to be outside, under that sky. He found the water bottle in his mother's bag and slipped out the door.

He first passed through the parking lot and slowed when he saw Father Leahy. Father was standing outside his room with another boy. Devon wasn't sure, but thought his name was Kevin. An eighth grader, a good kickball player. Devon had seen him in the yard. He was the only one who could kick the ball over the rectory. Father Leahy rocked backwards on his heels as he spoke to Kevin, and Devon saw Father Leahy smiling. The door to Father Leahy's room was just behind where they stood, open. Father Leahy seemed to look in Devon's direction, but neither smiled nor waved, so Devon didn't either. This wouldn't be the first time Father Leahy failed to notice him. Devon had felt his eyes skip over him in class, as if he were invisible.

Then Devon noticed a white pickup truck idling in the lot. The man who had performed at the plaza was inside the truck. He was wearing just a t-shirt, but Devon recognized the shape of his nose, his straight hair. He looked different in street clothes, Devon thought. Devon looked back to see Father Leahy turn and head into his room, and then Father handed an ice bucket to Kevin who walked to the ice machine behind the stairwell.

Devon could smell the exhaust filling his lungs. He crept closer to the truck. The young girl in the hat was inside too. The truck pulled out and drove away. Who else was in their family? Did they live nearby? He imagined a house, where they practiced their dance, spinning in the kitchen. The vehicle turned from the paved road onto a dirt road a quarter mile from the hotel.

Devon was no longer conscious of his feet moving beneath him. The ground blurred, his body kept time. He ran for as long as he could, but the truck was lost to him now, the clouds of dust he'd been following, gone. The desert absorbed his steps. He scanned the earth for shapes in the rocks. He lifted his eyes to the remaining light in the sky. The immense absence. The silence. The color. A lizard darted by. The cacti stood as sentinels, muted in life. He took the trail that disappeared around a hill, tracing the narrow line between land and nothingness.

He smiled at the gentle yellow flowers of the creosote brush that poked from over the precipice. They wriggled in greeting. He drew closer to see crevices that pocked a flat wall glowing red hundreds of feet below. His eyes lifted and he drew to the light, that sky again slipping its coat, revealing a new array of colors. He hungered for it. His steps quickened. His shoelace untied. His high tops and his calves were covered in a light layer of dirt, yet there was clarity to what he was doing. Everything was alive, purposeful. He felt dusk's strange energy in his limbs. He did not hear the helicopter in the distance. He thought only of the mysterious stillness of this place as he moved through it, its fugitive beauty.

When he'd walked until the verge of darkness, he sat on a jagged rock and drank the rest of the water. That's when he felt cool air. He turned in its direction and saw a dark mound the color of earth, hidden among the cottonwoods. He heard the song of a whip-poor-will and he wondered how he had never heard it before, as if everything had only just been transmitted to him on a frequency he could receive. He crawled in and let the coolness wash his eyelids. The dark smelled of must. On the ground, he sat in that stillness and took off his sneakers. He freed his toes, wriggling his feet into the sandy dirt, covering them, moving in circles. He was on his own. He got up and spun in a blur. He bounced and shook his body. He tossed his weight from side to side, mimicking the dancers. Every few beats, he'd make himself freeze in mid-step. Then he resumed the dance, drunk on agency. Death to that cord that had wound around him.

Rita stepped out of the bath, cracked open the door. She didn't hear anything. It was unlikely Devon was reading. He'd be watching t.v. or playing a game.

"Devon," she called. She wrapped a towel around herself and peered out the door into the hotel room. "What are you doing?"

Her steps quickened to the window. She grabbed her cell phone. It was 5:02 pm.

She dressed quickly. Outside she scanned all of the slow moving tourists at the edge of her vision. She walked briskly around the perimeter of the hotel. Her breath grew shallow. She checked in the lobby, in the restrooms, at the vending machines, in the bar, around the parking lot. She asked the desk manager, the waiters, several patrons in the lobby, the students she saw, but no one had seen Devon. She retraced hers and Devon's steps from earlier, the rim came into view and she stopped. The ranger had found her hysterical at the trailhead.

Day Two

There was no sign of him. Rita hadn't slept, but in the afternoon, she muffled her fear and hiked down 430 feet below the rim before becoming pale and weak. Father Leahy had escorted the other students home. He never returned. She had not been able to reach Richard, her ex. By late afternoon, there were radio calls, dispatches, checkpoints, flyers, text alerts, a local television crew. The dogs sniffed Devon's dirty clothes from a garbage bag.

Devon shook throughout the night but did not get up. A sharpness seized whenever he moved. Skin pinched. His throat was parched. The sharp edges of pain stilled him. An eternity passed. His breath faint, he slipped into a watery dream. Rowboats and small craft searched in the reeds along a wild shore. He did not know the meaning of any of this.

Day Three

The search resumed. It was Rita's new way of life. Perfect strangers surrounded her, embraced her, and looked after her. She had new energy though she hummed with emotional exhaustion. A beam shot through her. She had to be with the search party as it fanned out.

They found the water bottle first. There on the rock where Devon stopped and finished the last of it. Devon had traveled west, never descending. A man who worked at the gift shop and had joined the search on his day off saw the water bottle and picked it up. It was his third search since he was hired on the hospitality staff two years ago.

The canyon was candy-striped with shades of lilac and yellow, bathed in an improbable light. Gary from the gift shop kicked earth as he broke into a trot. He was the first to arrive in the darkened space. He later told the television crew something clicked when he saw the metal bottle and sat on the rock. He realized Devon must have sat on it too, then he saw the kiva's round form; it was the only shade in the area.

Devon was lying inside, knees to chest. The boat hat beside him.

Gary's eyes adjusted and startled at the sight of him, pushing away his first grim thought. He had been an EMT in another life, was well versed with venipuncture. Devon's hands and feet were covered in cholla spines. He'd seen this happen to stray pups in the desert. Gary put his ear to Devon's chest. The beat was there. He scooped him up.

Rita had run too and now she saw Gary as he emerged from the mound, carrying Devon's limp body in his arms.

Alive. They brought him back.

Over the years, Devon's mom would recount the story of how he disappeared—and she would rap him on head, snap a dishrag at him, when she told the story.

This one she'd say, *he tortured me.*

But Devon never bothered to recall the details of what had happened then.

Then, late one night in the bar near the station after work, he ran into an old friend, someone from Saint Augustine's. A conversation. Over beer. The friend had just heard of a death. Someone they overlapped with, *you knew who he was*, the friend had said.

"Didn't make it to 30. Died too young."

"You remember him. Soccer player," the acquaintance said.

Devon thought about it. Not much came up.

"Cmon, brown hair, *Kevin*. Played soccer, kickball, total athlete."

"Vaguely," Devon said. He felt a flash of heat.

Devon sat on the stool and rolled the tip of his napkin. Devon began pooling the memories he had of Kevin, glimpses formed slowly, dotted over a decade or more. There wasn't much. Then a frame came into view, like a clip from someone else's film. He felt himself in the desert. He drew back, felt something sharp catch in his throat. He took a quick sip of his beer, the liquid cooled it, and he lingered there, trying to rewind. Play it back.

It was Kevin, returning with the ice.

He stepped inside that room with the obscure light from the television animating it. Maybe a second of indecision, before he entered the room holding that bucket. Just then, Devon remembered Father Leahy's smile. Then the door closed.

CALL AND RESPONSE

AN ESSAY

LAURA COGAN

Recently a friend called and said she was losing hope.

In what, specifically, I asked. There are so many calamities, so many reasons. I didn't want to assume.

But in truth, I knew immediately what she was referring to—because, like me, this friend is Jewish, and because we have had so many other conversations.

"I'm having a tough time compartmentalizing my anger about the world right now," said another Jewish friend in January. We'd spoken before about lost friendships and tricky conversations with colleagues, about the vile online discourse, graffiti and vandalism at Jewish businesses, public events moved to zoom or cancelled, blacklists and boycotts, threatening crowds chanting hateful slogans.

"The propaganda is everywhere," lamented yet another Jewish friend in disbelief. A brilliant writer, she had spent the day arguing with bigots on social media. "I don't see how we are ever going to be able to correct these false narratives."

"We can't," I said. We are almost certainly never going to win the algorithmically enhanced (dis)information war. And it's become painfully clear that on this issue—the issue of what antisemitism is and whether it matters—we may not even be able to convince many of our friends and colleagues, people with whom we'd previously felt entirely aligned, to hear us. In this environment of self-righteous information silos and toxic sloganeering, what can I honestly say to console a friend who is losing hope?

—

I'm a words person. I understand storytelling to be the powerful force that it is. Human brains are wired to create and recognize patterns, and the patterns of narrative—from fable to religion to family lore to literary fiction and everything in between—are our most profound tool for making meaning out of the chaos of life.

Antisemitism is a particularly seductive kind of story: an adaptable conspiracy theory. The story it tells is never really about Jews—the subtext of the story is always determined by whatever a society most fears and reviles. If we try to break this powerful narrative spell by disputing it on a point by point basis with logic and facts, we have fallen into a trap because we have tacitly accepted the central premise of the antisemitic story—and we have thereby already lost. As the old saying goes, "*The antisemite doesn't accuse the Jew of stealing* because he thinks he stole something. He does it because he enjoys watching the Jew turn out his pockets." Instead, we have to tell our own story.

But storytelling only emerges out of the realm of the hypothetical when two parties are present and actively engaged: the teller, and the audience. The writer and the reader. A conversation. So the question arises, urgent and essential: is anyone listening?

"At the present moment," says historian Yuval Noah Harrari, "you can say that humans have the best, the most sophisticated information technology in history, and we are losing the ability to even talk with each other, and to listen, and to hold a reasonable conversation."

I've always wanted to believe that if I could find just the right language, I could break through any misunderstanding. But through experience—often painful, sometimes comedic—I've learned that this is not always the case; that a good conversation is not always available, and no matter how eloquent a speaker may be or how profound a story, there simply may not be an audience. Nothing is promised.

Which does, in turn, make any relationship, any organization, any community where we can foster actual dialogue especially significant.

—

Why is this subject so acutely fraught, so poorly understood, so hard to approach? Nothing about antisemitism makes sense until you realize that this intoxicating and shape-shifting global conspiracy theory presents a problem literally beyond words: it's a numbers problem, too.

Jews are less than half a percent of the global population. In the United States, Jews are under 2.5% of the population. What that means is that most people don't actually know what Judaism is, and therefore cannot possibly understand what antisemitism is, much less effectively examine their own bias—even *if* they were inclined to do that difficult work. Across the political spectrum, our allies are few and far between, and sometimes problematic in their own regard. Into this morass enters the internet, with devastating results.

"The amount of energy needed to refute bullshit is an order of magnitude bigger than that needed to produce it." This principle is called Brandolini's Law, or, more colloquially: The Bullshit Asymmetry Principle. To this eminently demonstrable axiom I'd add the following sub-rule, which we might call "Cogan's Conundrum": In the case of antisemitic bullshit, few people are equipped and willing to refute lies, and exponentially more are (for a variety of reasons, and with varying degrees of self-awareness) engaged in production. For example, the fact that much of the contemporary antisemitism now raging across college campuses is Soviet propaganda repackaged for a liberal Western audience is exhaustively well-documented and understood—in niche circles.

Perhaps when I told my brave writer friend that we can't defeat antisemitic rhetoric it sounded like disengagement or despair—it's not. I am, in my own quiet way, committed to speaking up, too. Like her, I refuse to normalize or rationalize this tsunami of antisemitism, and decline to take cover in the crowd. But not because I am working toward some goal—laudable though it would be—of ending antisemitism or correcting the public record or righting the sinking ship of public discourse. I'm not sure that such a thing is possible; certainly history does not suggest that it is. When I reject the prevailing narratives either aloud or privately, I think about that decision as a way of being in the world. Living with integrity. Living Jewish-ly, whatever that means to me. It's not a means to an end; it's an end unto itself. And I'm not doing it in the hopes of achieving anything beyond one honest moment followed by another and another.

Which has prompted me to consider a reframing of hope—that I shouldn't look for a *reason* to hope, a rationale that is persuasive and convincing to myself and others, a path to a better world that is logical and likely and achievable.

Instead, I should concern myself with living a hopeful life, *creating* a hopeful life. As the great Czech playwright Václav Havel wrote, "Hope is not prognostication. It is an orientation of the spirit, an orientation of the heart; it transcends the world that is immediately experienced, and is anchored somewhere beyond its horizons." So then: how do we orient ourselves toward hope—without lying to ourselves, or resorting to platitudes? Perhaps we start one conversation at a time.

—

Not that it's easy.

"You know," I suggested as gently as possible to a non-Jewish acquaintance who had said some odd if well-intentioned things, "being Jewish isn't *primarily* about the Holocaust." She looked at me blankly for a beat and then said, "Well, what *is* it about then?"

We looked at each other in disbelief at the chasm of confusion between us, and I wondered how to keep my answer simple enough that it could be intelligible across such a distance.

It was an uncomfortable moment—but illuminating, at least for me.

I told her that Jews are a 3,500 year old people ("עַם"), a type of group which defies modern categorizations of religion and ethnicity. Judaism is religious, cultural, and ethnic, I said. All true, what I told her. But later that night I lay awake thinking of how much more there is to say, to explain, and I wondered: what else should I have said? And would I ever get another chance?

—

I've had many of these unsettling conversations. There have been too many, and not enough. Sometimes they blur together in my memory. Sometimes the conversation I had the previous day runs through my mind over and over as I try to grasp the magnitude of the problem we're facing.

But I've noticed that my own ideas are often clarified by the engagement, despite the discomfort. It's not altogether dissimilar to what happens in writing: through articulating my thoughts, I not only discover more extensively what they are—I also revise and improve them.

I've noticed something else, too: whereas I might feel paralyzed or overwhelmed when left alone with my own thoughts, there is something in the nature of dialogue that (sometimes) brings out my better, more insightful self; something in the dynamic of conversation that solicits ideas and clarity and energy I did not know I had.

We need each other. Not as saviors, but because the call and response of dialogue can, if we let it, elevate, expand, and deepen our own thinking.

—

Sometimes, it must be said, there is no one to have that conversation with, no partner in discussion, no one to listen. Sometimes it seems as though you're about to have a conversation—but the other person turns away.

Several weeks after the massacre on October 7th, 2023, I went to lunch with a dear non-Jewish friend. As we walked to the restaurant on a bright San Francisco afternoon, he asked me how I was, and I told him how sad I felt about the war and the hate, and how isolated I felt in this grief. Yeah, he said, the world sure seems determined to be as divisive as possible right now. And then he changed the subject. He told me about a comedy show he went to the night before. It was pretty good, he said.

Call and no-response.

—

"Would you hide me?" has become a familiar thought experiment, from Nathan Englander's fiction to, more recently, a widely circulated video of Sheryl Sandberg tearfully describing posing that exact question to a startled non-Jewish friend. This is a conversation I am not interested in having. I think I can understand why American Jews might ponder this, and I have compassion for the fundamental insecurity that must underlie the impulse to ask.

But if I'm honest, I find this grotesque.

On so many levels, it's the wrong question, leading us all deeper into confusion. For one thing, the number of Righteous Gentiles in World War II was miniscule, so statistically speaking, we already know the answer to that question. Nevertheless, well-meaning non-Jews will, today, be confident they'd "do the right thing" in that imagined scenario because the "right thing" now seems, with the benefit of history and so much media, obvious. And, honestly, how could they answer otherwise? But there is nothing in this question ("Would you hide a Jew from Nazis?") to prompt anyone to understand much less push back against contemporary antisemitism, and as a result it is likely that any non-Jew will entirely miss the entire point of this pointless exercise.

Even worse: in asking this question of non-Jews, Jews themselves are setting the bar much, much too low. I know that may be a radical idea—and to clarify, I am not impugning the enormous bravery of the (very few) actual Gentile saviors. What I object to is the leading question posed to a self-gratifying end, rather than an honest conversation and direct engagement with the maelstrom of contemporary antisemitism. In fact, it opens a door to contemporary antisemitism—because everyone is comfortably convinced that *this* iteration is fundamentally different than *that* one. It isn't.

I do not wish to hide or be hidden—neither in a literal attic nor a figurative one constructed of assimilation and virtue signaling to reassure the crowd that I am one of the *good* Jews (and history shows us that what happens to the "bad" Jews always eventually happens to the "good" ones, too). I don't crave reassurance that a friend would hide me. My expectation of an authentic friend and ally is that they stand shoulder to shoulder with me publicly, in real time, rather than take easy satisfaction in imagining their valor in sepia-toned fantasies of the past.

—

The foundational prayer of Judaism is the Shema:

שְׁמַע יִשְׂרָאֵל יְהֹוָה אֱלֹהֵינוּ יְהֹוָה אֶחָד

Entire books can be—have been, will continue to be—written about the significance of this. A literal and strictly religious interpretation may begin and end at face value, with the command to worship one God and one God only. Author Dara Horn also frames the Shema historically, as a rejection of the tyranny of kings. In this sense, it has an ethical and political dimension. It is a declaration of human sovereignty—still a radical and threatening idea. As we are witnessing a near global slide into tyranny, this interpretation is as resonant now as ever.

I'm not especially observant, but I still find comfort in this prayer. And for my own idiosyncratic reasons I am also captivated by the opening word: שְׁמַע—*Hear!* Sometimes I think of it as a call to wake up, pay attention. I know this is not the literal meaning of the prayer. But it does some kind of unintentional work on me, reminding me: it is the endeavor of an entire lifetime to listen, to try to understand oneself and others.

It seems to me that in saying this prayer aloud we are speaking, of course, as we always are, to each other—and to ourselves. To God and to our community and also to the spark of the divine within us. We are exhorting and declaring, and in doing so we are also simultaneously fulfilling the command to *hear*—we are hearing ourselves, our own voice, and the voices of those around us.

Call and response seems as though it should require an unfolding in linear time, like a story, but the Shema collapses that notion: to chant this prayer is to begin to fulfill its central supplication.

—

Which brings me back, circuitously enough, to the idea that speaking up, and speaking truth, is an end in itself—and a way of orienting oneself toward hope. But I want to add this layer in, too: speaking *with* someone and hearing their voice, too, being in dialogue with a community—this is what really feeds the soul, sharpens the mind, broadens the heart. This is where hope may blossom.

It's essential on every level, from intimate relationships to building, maintaining, or salvaging the wildly imperfect project of democracy. "Democracy," Harari says, "is in essence a conversation between a large number of people… To have this conversation, you must have many voices."

—

Am I speaking up enough, doing enough? To be a relatively quiet, measured person in this cacophonous, extremist world is to wrestle at times with a sense of wrong-ness. I've wondered lately whether my temperament is an impediment to rising to the occasion. Which is a personal way of asking a philosophical question: what does this moment demand of us? Curiosity, I think, and compassion—and integrity. The intellectual integrity to challenge prevailing narratives.

Sometimes the right text, like the right conversation, finds you at just the right moment. Perhaps it was self-serving to find personal encouragement when I recently read these lines in Doris Lessing's enduringly relevant 1987 essay collection, "Prisons We Choose to Live Inside": "Every hour of every day you will be deluged with ideas and opinions that are mass produced, and regurgitated, whose only real vitality comes from the power of the mob, slogans, pattern-thinking. You are going to be pressured all through your life to join mass movements, and if you can resist this, you will be, every day, under pressure from various types of groups, often your closest friends, to conform to them."

And as though in answer to my question about whether I am doing enough, she writes nearly forty years ago: "Looking back, I see what a great influence an individual may have, even an apparently obscure person, living a small quiet life." I don't aspire to influence anyone, but I took this as validation, nonetheless, that there may be unexpected value in my minor contributions. That quiet voices matter, too.

—

I took a walk along the water with a new friend, someone I met in a roundabout way while seeking out Jewish community. She's a Bay Area native, has never been to Israel, and for most of her life, she's told me, she had internalized some antisemitic views and propaganda.

The massacre on October 7th and the immediate and pervasive groundswell of antisemitism across America and among her friends shocked her. She feels awake now, she often says. She likes to ask me questions about Israel, what it's like, why I feel safe there.

I love her questions. Hardly anyone ever asks me about Israel, or about antisemitism, even those who know my heritage and history. It's painful to wonder whether they might somehow imagine I am ashamed of my heritage, and so are tacitly ignoring it almost out of a sense of discretion. If so, they don't understand me at all. Is that misunderstanding my fault? Theirs? Neither?

That day on our walk I smiled as my new friend talked about our shared heritage, thinking how glad I was that we were together in this beautiful place, the bracing afternoon wind whipping our hair in our faces as the fog rolled in. I thought I felt happy. But there must have been some sadness on my face, too. What's wrong, she asked, prompting me to look at a shadowy thought that I hadn't yet articulated to myself or anyone else.

In this era of challenging conversations I've lost friends, and found new ones. Although it's easy to dwell on the losses, there is so much beauty in the gains. It is a gift to be seen, heard, and accepted—even if only by a few. But unlike some of my new friends who feel recently wakened to an ugly reality, I've been concerned about these issues my entire adult life. I've felt this storm coming for years. And for most of that time, I was almost entirely alone, at least in my social circles, where antisemitism is simply not considered urgent and the Middle East is poorly understood.

And now, I told her, I have these new friends, like you, friends who are in this with me—and I love that. But, you changed your mind once—about whether this all matters, about centering Jewishness and speaking up about antisemitism, even when it may cost us. And I worry, I guess, that you might change again and … leave me.

She stopped walking and pulled me into an embrace. We are not leaving you, she said, Ever. We are not going back.

Whether we are friends for life or for a season, what matters most to me about that exchange, what will endure in my own personal story of this difficult time regardless of what happens next, is that in that moment I called, and she responded.

LAIDLAW

A STORY

CHRIS FELICIANO ARNOLD

By August of 1904, the third summer of the new township, the fields had gone four months without rain. The temperature spiked at dawn, sun sizzled at midday, and by late afternoon, everything—the settlers, the livestock, the ground itself—was thirsty. Come evening, when the heat was finally tolerable, ranchers and their sons walked the corrals looking for animals that had perished of heat exhaustion during the day. The most common victims were sheep. Naturally slow to seek shade, they collapsed in the dust, where their corpses bloated within minutes. Lifting one into a wheelbarrow required several hands and the utmost care—one abrupt move and the animal would burst, leaking green bile from its mouth and anus. The boys, brushing flies from their faces, wheeled the dead to a side pasture and dumped the loads quickly. Bony packs of coyotes sniffed the remains each night but never partook.

At dusk following one of the hottest days of the drought, W. A. Laidlaw, the man whose name the township bore, lit the kerosene lamp outside his yurt, a simple canvas structure that served as the office for the Clear Water Irrigation Co-op, the first organization of its kind in Oregon. Then he rang a large silver bell and waited for some thirty men throughout the township to pull on their boots and walk, grumbling, to meet him. A tall, lean man with a salty-red mustache, Laidlaw wore a denim jacket, leather chaps, and a black hat no matter the weather, and sweat now beaded his face. The men assembled, eyeing a yellow slip of paper in Laidlaw's hand and speaking in low voices as the early moon cut the sky like a scythe.

"Gentlemen," Laidlaw said, holding the paper to the lamplight. "This telegraph has just been wired from Shaniko, and I promise you it cannot wait."

"Spare us another speech," said Nathaniel Sutherlin, standing beside his brother, Thomas, at the front of the crowd. It was they who, only days earlier, had led a small but vocal group of men in burning a crude effigy of Laidlaw in the fire pit just outside his office. The message was clear: Bring the railroad, or perish.

"Very well, I'll be succinct," Laidlaw said. "You have worked hard, you have sacrificed, and now you can tell your wives and children that Columbia Southern is bringing the future to Laidlaw."

Nathaniel snatched the notice from Laidlaw's hand. The men watched him read. "It's true," he said, removing his spectacles. "They're coming."

The assembly let loose a cheer and Nathaniel passed the slip around. Even those who could only pretend to read nodded in approval. At once, a flurry of questions:

"When exactly can we expect them?" Nathaniel said.

"And our shares?" his brother added. "What will they be worth now?"

"How soon till they need labor?" asked Joseph Walgamuth.

Laidlaw raised his hand to calm the crowd. "Tomorrow we'll all have business to attend to, I assure you. But tonight," he said, withdrawing a flask from his pocket, "tonight is for celebration."

The men whooped and whistled before dispersing to tell their wives. Laidlaw took a long, hot drink and wiped his mustache with the back of his hand. He retreated to his office to gather documents. Soon the air filled with laughter and pistol fire, and men convened at the central corral. Laidlaw closed the flaps to his yurt and returned to his table, where he continued to make preparations until he heard footsteps on the gravel outside.

"Mr. Laidlaw?" Walgamuth's brittle voice.

Laidlaw went to the door and opened a flap. "Yes, Joseph?"

Walgamuth stood, hat in hand, sweat glistening under the lamp glow. "I know you're busy, Mr. Laidlaw, but you ought to know, I've just got to tell you, I knew all along this would come together."

"I appreciate that sentiment," Laidlaw said. "Now why don't you go ahead and enjoy yourself some more."

"That I'll do. Bless you, Mr. Laidlaw."

Mr. Laidlaw, almost a decade earlier, had traveled by rail from Kansas City to Oregon City, determined to make a fresh start in time for the new century. That winter, his wife had fallen to influenza, and then he alone had remained with their son, just turned twelve. Laidlaw told the boy that if there was a hidden blessing to be found in their loss, it was the chance to make themselves over. A draftsman by trade, Laidlaw had spent all his working days drawing the estates of greater men. Out in Oregon he'd no longer be a bootlicker. What he lacked in capital, he could make up for in vision.

As a youth, Laidlaw had listened rapt to traders' stories of the great Oregon Trail, the vast prairie, the terrifying mountain peaks, the Indians hunting seemingly endless game, yet as he traversed the continent with his son, the only evidence of those tumultuous journeys was the occasional crooked grave site along the railway, each one a grim reminder that fortune didn't always favor the bold. His son spent the journey gazing out the window, leaving a nose mark on the glass whenever they passed a new town, and though Laidlaw couldn't shake the sense that they were arriving late to the parade, he felt satisfied that whatever lay over the next horizon might provide some meager balm for their grief.

That first spring in the Willamette Valley, a clubfooted stockman sold Laidlaw two hundred head of sheep with the assurance that there was still free grazing to be had in the Cascade high country. The high elevation there brought extremes, he allowed—scorching summers, cruel winters, and native fauna, brown and prickly, designed to thrive where moisture was scarce—but there was ample summer grass for the sheep, so long as Laidlaw didn't encroach on the buckaroos who would shoot to defend their cattle territories. And so with a pair of horses and a blue-eyed Australian shepherd, Laidlaw and his son drove their stock east through Willamette Pass.

It was a hot, dusty summer when they got to the high-desert country, but the animals contented themselves with the bunchgrass on the ridges. Laidlaw and the boy passed their days hunting, fishing, skipping stones across the creeks. At dusk the temperature sank, and in the crackle of the fire he felt the quiet presence of his wife, as if she had been following them the entire distance. She faded in the gray of morning, but Laidlaw began to believe that the worst was behind him.

In mid-October, the first snows fell, shallow enough that the sheep could still seek grass, and always followed by warm Chinook winds to melt the cold away. It had been a fine season. They had lost only twenty-one animals—a dozen to cougars, the rest to cliff sides. There would be profit enough from the wool clipping and butchering to cover the cost of winter grazing when they got back to the wet side of the state. The days grew colder and Laidlaw watched other ranchers begin their return journeys across the pass. He had the notion to sit tight just a couple of more weeks. No sense driving his herd back over any earlier than he had to, not when every dollar saved on winter grazing could be used to buy more stock the following spring. Against the warnings of the other ranchers, he waited.

It was the first of November when Laidlaw and his boy, thirteen by then, struck camp to hurry their herd west through the snow. In years to come, that date would hang over Laidlaw like a specter. If they had turned back a week earlier? Even a day?

Their third night crossing the Cascades, storm clouds wrapped the mountains in a steel cloak. Wind tore away their shelter and fire. By midnight the air had plunged below zero and his boy's teeth chattered so hard it seemed they might break. Laidlaw scrambled to capture one of his ewes. He slit the animal's throat and belly. Her steaming insides were their only hope for warmth. But before long the carcass itself was just a frozen mass. The boy had stopped shaking altogether, complaining now that he was too hot, too hot. Laidlaw wrapped the boy in his arms and shielded him from the wailing gusts. "Keep awake," he told the boy again and again, but there came a moment in the dark when he could no longer feel the boy's breath, when a terrifying cold rose up inside him, a sensation so powerful that, even years later, Laidlaw could not bring himself to utter the boy's name.

In the seasons to come, as Laidlaw traveled the state, scouting plots, studying irrigation methods, arranging deals with Portland brokers for claims to the high-desert wastelands, he did so with a dead-eyed determination to carve a settlement into that tough country. His son's death would not be in vain. His family hadn't made it, but others would, and they would thrive in a scrubland town bearing the name Laidlaw.

Thus the hand-painted blue and green signs, spread like seeds across the region. At a distance the announcements seemed like curious, colorful flowers growing everywhere one turned: the stagecoach trails from Shaniko to Plainview, Sisters to Oregon City; the riverbanks of the great Metolius; the trading posts along every westward route to the Willamette Valley; even the outhouses of taverns and brothels from the Snake River to the foot of the Cascades.

Each sign made the same promise, carefully lettered:

IRRIGATION
CREATES PROSPERITY
FROM WATER, SOIL, AND SUN!

see W. A. LAIDLAW
at the big bend in
the Deschutes river

Exhausted settlers who saw the notices felt a pang of promise that stayed with them along the river to the small yurt where W. A. Laidlaw waited. Laidlaw invited the men and their families inside, offered them water, a hot meal, a place to bed down for the night. When the women and children had gone to sleep, he offered the men whiskey and quail eggs, maps and divining rods, and, finally, a vision of the township: irrigation, railroads, a new age. He showed them crops of all kinds—barley, sweet beets, potatoes, strawberries—illustrated in his own charcoal sketches. Of course nothing in the high desert looked like the sketches yet. But with the right engineering, he promised, the river could be tapped to transform that landscape. Even the railroads knew it, and they were going to swallow up all the land. Laidlaw showed his visitors a map with the Columbia Southern seal, clear as day, in the upper right-hand corner, a red arrow pointing to the Deschutes River nearby. Those shimmering tracks would bring trade, mills, fortunes. There were visitors who called him a dreamer, a fool. But whatever in this life was too precious to lose, Laidlaw had already lost. The regard of strangers meant nothing to him.

For the believers there were agreements and signatures, handshakes and cigars, and by sunrise they had purchased shares in the Clear Water

Irrigation Co-op. Each day Laidlaw's silver bell summoned the men to the irrigation office to review maps, plot channels, and assign tasks. He led teams of men in clearing bitterbrush and juniper, readying the acreage for planting. Coaches rolled in with parts and supplies for constructing pumps and digging wells. A Klamath Indian and his white half-brother visited to share the secret of persuading water to flow uphill.

The settlers claimed and worked land of their own, erected simple frame dwellings, temporary structures that would suffice until the boom hit. During the second spring it seemed another wagon settled every week. With more hands, the townsfolk cultivated the volcanic soil, dark and mineral-rich from the explosion of the Cascades centuries earlier. Men hunted deer and elk in the dusty ridges nearby. Boys plucked trout like flecks of silver from the Deschutes River, cold and swift. Girls wandered barefoot in the rocky riverbeds, turning over stones, reaching into the murky swirls for crawfish; they returned home with wet dresses, bloody fingertips, pails brimming with russet creatures ready for the boil.

With time the irrigation channels grew more intricate. Soon professionals began to arrive, entrepreneurs eager to do business. Nathaniel and Thomas Sutherlin, a lawyer and a doctor from Ohio, erected a true office building the second summer. When the building was finished, the brothers spent their evenings on the front steps, Nathaniel perusing thick brown law books while Dr. Sutherlin whittled willow branches absentmindedly, watching the shavings curl at his feet. Michael Clancy spent the Indian summer building a trading post and fishermen's clubhouse. That fall he could be seen toying with a yo-yo as he waited for customers, and soon all the children of Laidlaw walked the paths with yo-yos spinning from their hands. Andrew Morton, a professor from back East, opened a two-room schoolhouse that doubled as a town hall, where at night the men gathered to drink and to chalk plans on the children's slates, exhausted from a day's hard work but fueled by the heat of their own dreams. On certain lonely evenings Laidlaw strolled past the schoolhouse door and lingered momentarily, just to absorb the fermentation, to hear the voices drifting across the settlement long after the sky had filled with fields of stars.

Then trade froze during the bitter winter of 1904. The settlement endured night after night of hard frost, but scarce snowfall left the faces of the Cascades bare, dashing hopes for a wet spring. Early lambs and calves were born steaming in the frigid dark and come sunrise the mothers persisted in licking the stiff, lifeless bodies of their young. Skeletal deer wandered the hills and buttes, desperate for grazing. Dr. Sutherlin killed a buck and strung it for cleaning, and when its organs spilled he pierced the stomach with the tip of his blade and discovered that the animal had been eating its own droppings. Michael Clancy took advantage of the awesome cold to sell every family in Laidlaw thermometers manufactured in Denver, and the men, bored with chopping firewood, argued daily whether the instruments, which lingered stubbornly near zero, could possibly be accurate. At the schoolhouse Professor Morton spent his lessons stoking the woodstove while the children shivered at their desks and practiced arithmetic on their cold tablets. There would be no new chalk until the trails opened. The professor broke sticks of chalk in half and in half again until the chalk was gone, and finally one day he led the children, with their tin buckets, down to the river. He sawed a hole in the frozen current and the children formed a bucket line to flood the central corral. Out walking the settlement later, Laidlaw leaned against the corral fence and watched the youngsters pass their arithmetic hour at play on the makeshift ice rink.

Only one child—the son of Joseph Walgamuth—remained at the schoolhouse, stacking wood for the professor. Young Ethan volunteered his efforts every day. The boy took after his father. Within a season of arriving in the settlement, the elder Walgamuth had constructed an animal hospital, a livestock market, and a feed shack. Of anyone in the township, it was Walgamuth and his son who saw most clearly Laidlaw's vision for the future.

Laidlaw remembered the bright morning that first spring when Walgamuth's wagon had rolled to a stop outside the co-op office. Laidlaw had been inside his yurt, shaving. He had splashed soap from his face, rinsed the red whiskers from his razor, and inspected his mustache in a hand mirror. He buttoned his shirt and donned his black hat and stepped out into the mild morning. A short, fragile-looking man stepped off a small wagon and limped toward the door. A woman and a little boy, both blond and freckled, hopped off after him and hitched their brown horses to a post.

"Are you Mr. Laidlaw?" the man asked. The tip of his nose looked badly burnt or bitten.

"Yes, sir, I am," Laidlaw said, holding open the canvas flap. "Please. Come in. Make yourself at home." The man nodded at his wife and little boy and the two went to unhitching and brushing the horses. "And your name?" Laidlaw asked the boy.

"Ethan."

"Welcome, Ethan." It had been a long time since anyone had given the boy a haircut and a good scrubbing. On his belt he kept a small knife, and the worn leather sheath made it clear he took every opportunity to use the blade during chores. There was a burning in Laidlaw's throat and he coughed into his fist. "You take good care of those horses," he said.

"Yes, sir."

Inside, Laidlaw pointed Walgamuth to a small table in the center of the yurt. He filled two tin cups with whiskey. Laidlaw watched Walgamuth lift the cup with the thumb and ring finger of his right hand. His other fingers were missing at the first knuckle.

"Frost," Walgamuth said, wiggling his half fingers.

Laidlaw knew well enough about frost. He wondered whether Walgamuth had buried any children on his journeys. A softness in the man's eyes revealed that, no, he had not. Laidlaw let the man enjoy his whiskey and the pleasant breeze through the open flap.

"We saw signs posted back up the river a ways," Walgamuth said after a time.

Laidlaw moved the cups and the lantern aside to make space for his charcoal sketches. The man leaned over the table, scrutinizing the illustrations and accompanying diagrams. Laidlaw could tell by the movement of Walgamuth's eyes that he could not read and so he pointed at the sketches one at a time, explaining the purpose of each plot of land, the irrigation routes, the crop rotations, the plans for a reservoir.

"Columbia Southern is just around the corner," Laidlaw said, standing. "The whole world is one train track away." He led Walgamuth outside to see for himself. The boy was still brushing the horses and the animals took long drinks from the water trough. Laidlaw invited

Walgamuth's wife to join them. Blackbirds pecked at a puddle of water at their feet. Laidlaw pointed to the fields in the middle distance, flat and dry. Already that morning a dozen men with shovels and picks stood waist deep in fresh canals, digging. Just one year prior, Laidlaw had spent hours alone in this very spot, sketching the landscape, studying how the contours might make for good plots, how the ridges might be terraced, how channels could navigate the fields like veins feeding the needy crops. Now as Walgamuth held the sketches and looked over the land, a river of words flowed from Laidlaw's mouth, filling the dry canals, and as Laidlaw pointed along the horizon it was as if his sketches unfurled across the landscape, and Walgamuth, too, seemed to see the lush fields, the crops tussling in the breeze, acres of prosperity for every man, woman, and child, all the way to the foot of the Cascade Range. Out in the canals the men paused in their digging to gaze back at the new family.

"By the grace of God," Walgamuth told his wife. "We've made it."

Now, this harsh afternoon, as Laidlaw watched the youngsters skate the icy corral, young Ethan glanced at him from the woodpile behind the schoolhouse and held his eyes a moment before carrying on with his chore.

The first hot days of the impending drought were still weeks away, and nobody, not even Laidlaw with all his vision, had any notion that spring would come rainless and then surrender to a summer of punishing heat, clouds gathering on the horizon, dark but never dark enough, shadows drifting forever east, leaving behind nothing but cracked earth. With no snowmelt to come and no rain, the river would run low—the fishing poor, the flow of irrigation pathetic. Laidlaw Township would dream of heavy clouds that summer but wake each morning to a merciless and vacant sky. The residents kept their eyes upward, to the promise of rainfall, but by the middle of June, blue was the color of pain. The Deschutes had barely the strength to slip through the riverbed stones. With so little water the spring crops failed. Laidlaw rang his bell continuously, it seemed, to call the men to his office to dispense some news, some semblance of hope, but ultimately there was no word yet from Columbia Southern. In August, thirst, desperation.

But that afternoon, as Laidlaw watched young Ethan carry an armload of split wood into the schoolhouse, he could not know the pestilential winter was only the start of his troubles. He straightened his hat and returned to his yurt. At the office table, he examined his sketches, sorted through his contracts, went back to the business of making sure the future knew where and when to arrive.

It was when the Sutherlin brothers gathered the mob to light their effigy that Laidlaw knew his time had expired. Seated on his cot, he had endured the shouted threats as smoke from the burning figure penetrated his canvas walls. No good options occurred to him in the days following. And so that second week of August, the night he had shared his telegraph from Shaniko, the night he had declared that the future was finally on its way, Laidlaw packed his horse with a small bag of essentials, his charcoal sketches, and six pouches of water. As the men of the settlement drank themselves dizzy, Laidlaw poured kerosene throughout the yurt, over the table, over the folders of shareholder records, over the many pages of failed and forged correspondence with Columbia Southern. There were too many papers to carry, not enough time to bury them, not enough water in the river to wash them away. By destroying those documents, Laidlaw felt, he could at least relieve the settlers of the liens on their land, offer them an opportunity to leave this place free and clear. On his way out the door, he struck a match and held its glow to his face briefly before dropping it to the floor.

Laidlaw mounted his horse and flew down the long main road, past the last fences in the settlement, then east. Behind him, sparks leaped, multiplied, gained altitude in the breeze. Before long the roofs of nearby structures ignited. Patches of dry weeds smoked and flared, and fire spread to the hay bales around the central corral. Soon the blaze touched the only real building in town, the Sutherlin office. By then the men were waking their families, shouting, scrambling for buckets and shovels.

Some three miles upriver, Laidlaw brought the horse to a halt. Through the darkness across the fields, orange shapes wavered on rooftops and fences and now in the dusty juniper bushes alongside the road. He'd intended that only his office burn, and for a moment a heavy sickness compelled him to turn back to help extinguish the flames. But in a way, he envied these men their chance to start anew. They hadn't lost everything. Perhaps now they would wake from his dream and take their wives and sons and daughters over Willamette Pass, settle in a valley where they could again feel rain on their faces. Laidlaw spurred the horse and rode harder, south, along the river trail.

In the settlement the men felt only flames. They bound their necks and mouths with wet handkerchiefs and attacked the blaze with shovelfuls of dirt, and the iron handles branded their palms. Boys fetched half-full pails of water from the thin river, working in teams, water sloshing as they hurried back along the path. Yellow waves flooded the fields and washed over the dry, dusty cheat grass. Dogs barked frantically. The women and girls released the sheep and goats and horses from the corrals, herded the confused animals down the smoky roads. The moon hung over the tree line all the while.

Laidlaw knew he would be hunted the moment the men had saved their homes. Heat rose from the shadowy dust on the trail as he pushed the horse at a hard gallop along the riverbank. A pair of porcupines wobbled lazily from the brush. The horse reared. Laidlaw clutched the reins. A low-hanging juniper branch smacked his head, gashing his brow, and the horse charged between the two porcupines as Laidlaw's black hat fell to the ground.

It was another mile upriver before the horse settled and Laidlaw dismounted. His brow was sticky and he splashed water on the throbbing wound. No time to go searching for the hat. He led the animal to the water. Frogs gurgled in the tall grass. The horse bowed, shoved its muzzle between the river stones, and drank. Dust still lingered on the trail behind them. Laidlaw filled his deerskin canteen, took a long gulp, and dipped the canteen again. The horse snorted and stomped impatiently. The moon planted specks like white seeds in the dark current and they trickled over the stony bottom. Laidlaw heard his heart pound over the sound of the moving water. His dream flickered one last time. The river—artery of the settlement; the railroad—shimmering tracks along its banks. He'd wished to reward the township families for everything they'd suffered and lost. But surely they must have known that no man could protect them from the weather.

Coyotes yipped, chasing after something in the trees.

Laidlaw climbed back on his horse, snapped the reins, and forced the animal into the black water. The horse walked delicately, hooves struggling on the jagged bottom. On the opposite bank, Laidlaw rode south once more. Even from this expanse smoke tinged the air. How many men, how many good dogs could the Sutherlins array against him? The horse had already sweated twice. Laidlaw swiped his palm along his brow and smeared a dark patch of blood on his jeans. As the horse loped, he looked back across the river at the trees lining the bank, at their twisted shadows and branches. In the distance, the butte, a giant silhouette. He let the horse dip down for one last long drink and then rode hard up the trail another mile before crossing back again. He crossed twice more, and by then, as the sun peered over the horizon, lighting up the gray bare peaks, the horse was shuddering beneath him.

—

The dogs had quit barking. With nothing left to do but let the fires run their course, the men rested. The Sutherlin building, once sturdy, had been reduced to a charred skeleton. Ashy pages of textbooks fluttered from the second-story windows like black feathers. The rest of the structures in town had fared no better. The schoolhouse, the tavern, the trading post—all strewn along the road like burnt match sticks.

"No sense fighting for what's left," said Nathaniel. "Let's see how many horses we can round up."

Throughout the commotion, the men had felt the weight of W. A. Laidlaw's absence. Thomas Sutherlin had already saddled his horse and sheathed his rifle. Professor Morton and Michael Clancy stood at the schoolhouse, picking through the remains with shovels and pitch forks, the losses clear even in the predawn. Clancy's wife stood beside him, cradling their newborn twins, who by some miracle had slept through the chaos. The men banded together and found Walgamuth, on his knees outside his decimated home.

"We need your dogs," Nathaniel told him.

"My rifle. It's in there," he said, pointing to the stock of his weapon glowing hot in a coil of cinders.

"We have others," Thomas said. "Now let's get moving."

A tiny strip of pink light edged the horizon. Thomas lit a torch and led the weary men down the river trail as the hounds ran ahead, noses to the ground. A few miles later the dogs circled Laidlaw's black hat and seized a scent, and the men followed, Thomas's torch casting gold on the river surface. The horses thundered on the trail. It wasn't long before the dogs paused, trotting back and forth near the riverbank. The men stopped to water the horses. Already heat rose from the dust, and the Sutherlins, their cheeks still blistering from the fire, cursed it.

"Son of a bitch crossed here," Nathaniel said.

The dogs' scent was true, and the men followed them back and forth across the river. It was only when the hounds turned off the river trail completely that Clancy suggested maybe they had gone mad with heat.

"He's long gone," Clancy said.

"Unless he'd only have us think he's gone," Thomas said. He pointed his torch at the butte, a dark heap in the distance. An owl hooted, a phantom leaping from tree to tree.

"Ain't a drop of water up there," Walgamuth said.

"Understand how this man operates," Professor Morton said. "He wants us to ride past."

"Professor," Nathaniel said, "you and Walgamuth and Clancy take the dogs around the butte. Keep them worked up and noisy. My brother and I will ride up the back side and surprise him. When he heads down your way, you boys be waiting."

"What makes you so sure he's up there?" Walgamuth said.

"He's made fools of us once," Thomas said. "Sure enough, he thinks he can do it again."

"We're wasting time with this debate," the professor said.

The torch hissed as Thomas extinguished it in the river. The professor led his men around the butte, hounds baying through the shadows of the trees. The Sutherlin brothers rode to the trailhead on the opposite side, where in the blue-gray dust they discovered the lingering imprints of horseshoes they were looking for. Even at sunrise their horses worked up a noontime sweat trudging switchbacks up the hill. Halfway up the brothers surveyed the settlement in the middle distance. Pillars of smoke drifted into the lightening sky. From the other side of the butte came the faint barks of Walgamuth's hounds.

"Figure he knows what we're up to?" Thomas said.

"Sure as the devil."

At the summit the mountains to the west were gray in the rising sun. Laidlaw stood shirtless in the shade of a thick juniper and poured water from his canteen into his hand. He held his palm to the horse's mouth and let the animal drink. When he saw the Sutherlins approaching, he made no effort to run or reach for his gun.

"I have a peculiar feeling," said Laidlaw, oddly calm, "that nothing I have to say will be of much interest to you gentlemen." Thomas drew his revolver and fired at Laidlaw's kneecap. "Goddamn!" Laidlaw called out, and dropped to the ground. "Goddamn goddamn goddamn!—" Nathaniel struck Laidlaw's mouth with the butt of his rifle. The brothers went to work binding his arms and legs with a length of rope and together heaved him over his horse.

Once down the butte, they allowed their weary animals a pause for long drinks at the riverbed. Laidlaw groaned.

"Suppose we better call the others," Nathaniel said.

"They're going to want some time with him," his brother said. "Walgamuth, especially."

"I imagine so." Nathaniel lifted his rifle and fired three shots into the air. Soon the hounds howled through the trees. When Laidlaw, twisted on his saddle, saw the men approach, his eyes widened and he curled himself into a ball. The men dismounted, hauled Laidlaw to the ground, and went after him with their boots and fists until they needed a drink.

"That's enough now," Thomas said. "We bring him back alive."

Energized from the capture, the party galloped fast toward the settlement. The day grew hotter and Laidlaw coughed dust and blood as the saddle jarred him. They reached the remains of Laidlaw's yurt and dumped him there in the grit. Men, women, and children alike surrounded the group to watch Laidlaw writhe.

Professor Morton recovered an ashy, silver bell from the cooling embers of the co-op office. "These children ought to get washed up," he told the crowd. "Not one of you returns until you hear the sound of the bell." The parents agreed, and begrudgingly the older children led the youngsters away. The settlers circled Laidlaw, their eyes bloodshot, faces soiled and sweaty in the rising heat. Women spat at him and kicked soot. The men dealt blows until they were satisfied or exhausted. Finally the crowd looked to Nathaniel for any guidance the law could provide as to what should happen next.

"It's a day's ride before we can get the sheriff out here from Prineville," he said. "If the sun finishes him by then, so be it."

Laidlaw was dragged to the far pasture and bound to a juniper trunk. Once the knots had been cinched, the restless crowd returned, ashen-faced and silent, to the central corral, where the professor grasped the silver bell, took a deep breath, and rang it steadily. The sound echoed through the trees, from which the children, emerging now, had overseen the beating. Together with their mothers and fathers, they trudged wordlessly down to the banks to scrub themselves clean in the water.

The sun moved slowly across the sky. At dusk, the howls of coyotes stirred Laidlaw from his daze. It was as if his body were filled with splinters of glass. He could not be sure if he was burning or freezing. He passed his tongue over cracked lips, and through one swollen eye glimpsed figures across the pasture, sifting still through the smoldering remnants. Above them, clouds assembled into one dark mass, and as he fell unconscious, he dreamed of sudden thunder and the first, fat raindrops thrumming the desert floor.

In the pitch of night Laidlaw woke and peered through bloated eyes at great bulbous flashes of heat lightning, silent on the horizon. Across the pasture came the glare of a lantern, hovering like a ghoul above the dust. He braced himself to be finished off. He called out, a cry for mercy that spilled from his broken mouth as one low moan. The lantern drew closer and in the sickly glow he recognized the boy's face.

"It's me, Mr. Laidlaw," the child told him, and raised a cold canteen to his lips. "Drink."

PART TWO

NEWLIT CREATIVE WRITING WORKSHOPS 2025:

Albany High School; Concord High School; East Bay Center for the Performing Arts; Emery High School; Girls Inc of Alameda County; Leadership Public Schools Hayward; Northgate High School; Mt. McKinley High School, Contra Costa County Juvenile Hall

WRITING FROM STUDENTS, INSTRUCTORS, ALUMNI

—

BONNIE BONETTI-BELL FELLOWS & WORKSHOPS: UNIVERSITY OF CALIFORNIA, BERKELEY, ENGLISH DEPARTMENT

Camille Santana Considine, Edil Hassan, Drew Kiser, Ryan Lackey, Laura Ritland

—

IRIS STARN FELLOWS & WORKSHOPS: SAINT MARY'S COLLEGE OF CALIFORNIA MFA CREATIVE WRITING PROGRAM

Isa Maloof, Genay Markham, Courtney Pazin, Rayjon Briscoe Young

DID YOU HEAR HER DROWNING?

ZARA SHARZA

NORTHGATE HIGH SCHOOL

They look like prey.
They're scared.

Except that Scarlet is no stranger to fear. No stranger to running or leaving. When she was eight, Mom got a little too mad and Jade (always the big sister, the protector, the savior, and what was Scar supposed to do except be saved) got scared. She grabbed Scar and little brother Alex and they left Dad and Mom and the screaming behind, ran far, too far, into the woods and got lost. The police found them two miles deep into the Pennsylvania forest, curled together at the bottom of a flowering dogwood tree. Like the ashy casts of Pompeii. Three Graces, three Muses, three Fates. Three siblings, each with nightmarish songs in their minds. Scarlet is going to sing hers until the day she dies.

They look like angels.
They're almost saints.

Except that Ashlynne is all the wrong kinds of unholy. She doesn't smile when she gets called pretty. She doesn't give people the benefit of the doubt. She meets boys in back alleyways (teeth like wolves, kisses like fire, hands like ice, lingering touches like atomic smoke) and learns their names after learning their bodies. Her skin betrays her guilt; a tapestry of scars for every name she gets called. A white line on her forearm every time she is betrayed, a bruise on her hip for every fingerprint left behind. She just tries too hard. Attracts too much attention. It's not her fault. She's like Psyche, forced through trial after trial, the price of being beautiful. She's the participation trophy, the guaranteed win. Everyone gets to have her.

They look like martyrs.
They're memorialized.

Except that Violet is not sure anyone will ever know her name. She's holding knife up to her skin, the end a whisper awa. The only people who will ever know are the ones who made her (broken, bruised, standing at the kitchen window, the scent of her favorite candle in the air, the flame extinguished). If she does this will die unknown, never seen, never understood, and that makes her set the knife down just as the first drop of blood bubbles. Violet wants to survive but she also wants to be gone and she isn't sure which is scarier. She's like Eurydice, the doomed maiden: trying to escape, but love is synonymous with death.

They look like prisoners.
It's just in their heads.

Except that Kayla has seen it all. She's watched firsthand as girls set themselves aflame with lighters forged in self-hatred, watched light fade from eyes. She takes pride in being the oldest resident of the ward, the confidant, the girl with wings. Ready to protect. She knows Scarlet yearns for a family long abandoned, and she knows Ashlynne wishes she'd never taken James McLeod's hand, and she knows Violet awaits a day perfect for Death's horse. She is Apollo, god of prophecy; she always knows how these girls will end.

Except no one could predict it, when it happened.
No one could save her.

Ashlynne wasn't sure who found her. Maybe it was Scarlet—she screamed first—or maybe it was Kayla, who ran for help. Or maybe Violet had seen the blood dripping from her own wrists and knew she had only had minutes, maybe she had started screaming with the gravity of what she'd done. Maybe the fear of being gone had finally gotten to her; maybe she was just too terrified.

Except it took them three minutes to reach the bathroom.
It took three minutes for Violet to stop.

ANALI PASCUAL

GIRLS INC OF ALAMEDA COUNTY

"Dos barras de chocolate, el anhelo de un corazón"

Me siento confundida sin salida
Me siento culpable sin razón alguna
Siento romperme en mil pedazos
I YEARN for something, though its form eludes me.
I YEARN for HIM and would like to know if we can be something more.
I want to understand how I truly feel.
No me detiene su amor, No me detiene el temor
Me detiene la culpabilidad de saber que esto no lo aceptarán
como debe ser
Qué haría falta para salvar este abismo?
¿Quizás una palabra, o dos almas valientes sin miedo?
Me pregunto si algún dia sabrás lo que pasa por mi cabeza
If you hold me in your thoughts as I do you in mine.
If one day you will understand what I've cried for, despite it
meaning nothing.
Si algún día podré estar entre tus brazos.
Let our love be dark and sweet like chocolate's embrace,
Like dark chocolate truffles, we tempt with our grace.

Don't let age be an obstacle to what we can have
Así que disfrutemos de este momento.
In the electric silence when our eyes collide,
A language unspoken, yet whispered inside.
Anhelando conversar, pero la distancia nos separa,
This unrequited love shadows our light.
¿Hasta dónde podemos vagar, entrelazados en sueños?

Beyond just a hug, where our hearts are aligned?
Más que besos, dónde las almas se atreven a vagar,
In the depths of our longing, we seek a way back,
To a home where our hearts won & feel the lack.
A place that's just ours, where love can roam free,
Where it's always just us, together we'll be.

TWO POEMS

VIOLET FERREIRA

GIRLS INC. OF ALAMEDA COUNTY

The Road to Angkor

Surrender your steps to the ghosts of hi-hats and toms
Strain your shadowy eyes past the tendrils of heat that lick the grain,
Find an apsara
She twists painfully
Painfully slow towards the golden glint of a crowned temple
Hands bound, you must feel the rhythm in the soles of your feet
Follow the 16th notes that ricochet in your rib cage, humming pulse guiding you
Guiding you towards a lost city illuminated in saffron luster
When the weight grows too heavy to bare, finally lay your scythe to rest
Ignore the wild roar
The wild roar that commands the sickle to your fist laden with shreds of red string
A voice, of lethal decree urges you to turn your back
Turn your back on your kin and credence
Shelter your ears and pay him no mind
Aching chest and heavy hands, plow past your fields one last time

The Ghost of Wisteria Grove

A tall sunken house resides on a lot past the orchards down West, I must brave my
stride
Towards a menagerie of vines and boarded wood, this will be my next quest

Children cower at the moans puncturing ballads of breeze
Lulls of hymns give way to shrieks of horror,
I ignore the sedating wards that desperately cling
Blankets of violent purple assault placid planks
It is here that I get a chill that I can't quite shake
A foundation of rot, the home lives on a slant
Hesitating steps, I must trudge onwards
Yet my feet refuse to move, tethered by root and plant
Magnificent fortress of vine and dirt, the dwelling tires at the top of a cliff
A pleading soprano echoes from the great expanse
I hang precariously, ligaments giving, I begin to drift
A hand meets mine, an invitation to a tranquil dance
Inquisitive touch turns to a desperate pull
She whispers to me, unleashing a mortal arsenal,
Tongue of venom, she employs her greatest tool

"Come close and we may begin to fuse
When faced with a reflection, let me see you
My eyes lay sullen, empty, in search of release
I'll be your sanctum and you'll be my peace."

ALEXIS MONTIFAR

NORTHGATE HIGH SCHOOL

Poem

Just this morning, I faced a decision:
two flowers entwined in one pot
I knew I should pull them apart
with precision,
delivering the freedom sought.
Intricate roots refused dissection,
slow despair,
crowded and crammed with affection,
perhaps beyond repair.
These flowers with roots
all spun together,
the torture of change,
To flourish under new weather
parted like lovers,
estranged.

BALANCE BEAM

YARELIE

ALBANY HIGH SCHOOL

THE DARKNESS OF A MAN'S WORLD

A collaborative poem

K. EMANUELLE MENDOZA, EIFA LAM-TRIPLETT, ENAYA BUKSH, SOPHIA RUIZ-BRAZ

LPS HAYWARD

This poem was composed by four 9th grade students at LPS Hayward on the first day of our poetry class. The students practiced nonstop writing to various music, then chose their favorite lines, which they put into a bag without putting their names on them. Then the lines were chosen out of the bag and the students each had a chance to put their hands on the poem and arrange it in the order they found most fitting. The poem has been lightly edited while keeping the students' original order.—Isa Maloof, Iris Starn Fellow

Building a bond with earth,
to build a relationship with –
despite its struggles

Dark, light,
like the sun was
beside me.

The darkness of another
man's world is
what one always sees

before the sun in front of
them. How can you blame them?
I wish you understood more, but you don't

I wish you understood more, but you don't
Even though you might feel afraid,
you shouldn't because

God will help from the darkness
God can bring you into the light,
God loves you

Even when I try to write
the bare minimum in
essays I can't because I can never think

Everyone seems so sure
As if one's optimism is
word to live by

Sometimes I struggle with
incorporating poetry,
daily,
but mostly in my essays.

MUSICA MON AMOUR

LINA IHADDADENE

EMERY HIGH SCHOOL

Linda is a waitress working at a little restaurant near the beach in California. She lives in the suburbs, but her house is a small, unattractive dwelling situated between the more elegant homes. She feels the people's eyes roaming over her brown house with a non-lowered mower whenever they walk by, the cars slowing down to check who could possibly afford living in the suburbs, yet have such an ugly, unmaintained house.

She usually doesn't care much, it was her grandfather's house, he passed away during the summer, and since he didn't have any other grandchildren and her parents died in a car accident when she was in college, she was the only legacy left. After his death, she decided to move into his house, not knowing exactly what it looked like. She never really knew her grandfather; her parents kept him at arm's length and barely mentioned him. The only thing she knew about him was his love for music, a love she shared with him. She always knew she wanted to be a singer, yet her parents always told her to get a "real" job; it was as if they wanted to keep her away from her love for music.

June 21st, the longest day of the year, and our little Linda has to work from sunrise till sunset. And the morning had already started badly, as she got out of bed with a cold feeling, the window wide open, sending in fresh and dusty air, which was unusual considering the time of year. All she could think of was closing the window before sleeping. "Must have been broken during the night." She didn't know much about it and continued with her day.

She always starts off with music blasting in the house while getting ready. But for some reason when she went down she heard a faint melody coming out of the vinyl player, she thought it might be defective, but while approaching it she realizes that there was no vinyl and it was turning round, and round on the air, a shiver went through her spine, she looks around a bit startled since she had only been there for a couple of days and yet it isn't the first time something like that happens, she always had a weird feeling in that house, she was never alone, but when she puts on music, which is ninety per cent of the time she feels watched, like she is giving a concert to a whole crowd, yet she goes past it and ignores it. But this morning was different, somebody was there she didn't knew who, but she was definitely not alone she look around quite as a mouse, paying attention to every single detail around her, she stays like that for a whole two minutes, wanting to make sure no one was in her house, or rather, her grand-father house. After that, she went on with her day, got ready, and headed out, all with no music since the morning's events were still in her head.

Once at work, it seemed like a typical workday, nothing out of the ordinary. The day was long and tiring; all she could think about at the end of the day was taking a warm bubble bath. On her way, she realized the city was still full of people, as it was a Saturday night, but for some reason, her street was pretty quiet. "Huh, I guess there is a reason why they call it Fear Street after all," she told herself as she was walking home. As soon as she said that, she heard a laugh right behind her, almost as if the person was whispering in her ear, making sure she heard him. It sounded old and raspy, as if the person had smoked cigarettes their whole life. She turns around in a quick motion, yet nothing . . . nobody is in sight. She was alone, alone with a smell of cigarette in the air, which she had never smelled in her neighborhood before, but she knew the only smoker around was her grandfather.

Once home, she went directly to the bathroom. Trying to forget what had just happened, she puts on some music and turns on the water. She serves herself a glass of wine and gets in. The feeling of being watched grew even more intense; she felt uneasy and uncomfortable. She decides to get up and rinse herself off, but while she tries to get up her music got louder, and louder, she hadn't paid attention because of all the thing reminiscing in her mind but she had never heard that song before, it was certainly not in her playlist since it consisted of whispers getting deeper and louder, almost like they were in the same room as her. She panics, tries pushing herself up, but she keeps getting pulled back into the bathtub. She tries screaming, but all her sounds become whispers. And the more she debated with the water, the deeper she got pulled. She was slowly drowning, slowly fading away with only a whisper as her last word...

"Why…" June 22nd newspapers titled: "Another victim of the fear house, twenty-two-year-old Linda drowned in her bathtub, the same one that killed her grandfather."

"They said they heard whispers all around the house, you know," said Rosa with a scared look.

"Oh, come on! Don't tell me you believe those old granny stories," said Tilly as the floor creaked under the two girls' light and cautious steps. Tilly steps on the glass, causing both girls to scream.

"Haha, look, here is the only thing that is likely to kill us in this house," she says as she picks up the glass.

"Be careful with that, it looks sharp." As Rosa said that, Tilly cut herself open, causing her to hiss in pain. As soon as the drop of blood hit the floor, a faint whisper was heard in the Air. "Why?" The girls ran out of the house screaming for their lives and never looked back.

POEM

ERICA MATIAS

GIRLS INC OF ALAMEDA COUNTY

Our Walk to the Train

The wind blowing through my long hair and hers
But her hair is tied in a low bun, with her traditional headband
Her care reassures me to wear my covering to prevent sickness
Side by side she walks with me, for she shares her worries about Son
The sky is gloomy, I tell her, I will talk to him
Her love is soft and reassuring
Her support I can't thank enough
Do your best and focus she says
I can't begin to explain more how she wants me to excel
I walk through the two-sided doors and wave goodbye
She slowly starts to fade
I look out for her again and I see her
I see her modesty and beautiful smile
I wait and wait for the train
As it arrives I look for her again and say one more last goodbye

WITHIN US

KALAIJAH WALKER

EMERY HIGH SCHOOL

The smell of petrichor filled my nose as the ten other campers followed the trail, leading us to our camping ground. My eyes set on the cabins, which would be housing a total of thirty kids. Children from all over the world come to Camp Tallulah, located in the National Forest of Tennessee.

"Boys to the cabin to the east, girls to the cabin located to the west," the tallest counselor exclaimed.

We dispersed to our respective cabins. The bed located near the back of the cabin caught my eye. The floor beneath me creaks with each step I take, and the noises and cobwebs tell me this cabin has been here for a while. The chatter in the cabin dies down the moment I focus on my thoughts. Shadows swarm me, no, not shadows, death. A rush of blood from my toes to my head overwhelms me, knocking me forward. "Alexandria," a thunderous voice hits my ears. Shock hits my bones, making my spine curve, "ALEXANDRIA," I fling upward, locking eyes with the cabin leader. The sun hits his light golden hair, making it shine right into my eyes. I take multiple breaths before answering the tall figure standing over me.

"I need you to walk with me," He says.

I inhale sharply, all I wanted was to rest for a few after the long journey here. I stand, walking out of the creaky cabin with Trevor, considering that's what his name tag says.

Trevor and I cross the line that separates the wilderness from the camp, and the smell of fresh air immediately fills my lungs, making me feel more expansive. This is precisely where I am supposed to be. I hear a crunch to the left of me and remember I'm not alone. The realization that I'm alone with a strange man hits me.

"Where are we going? And why are we here?" I finally ask. My eyebrows raised in clear suspicion. I watch the back of his head as I wait for him to answer. He turns around so quickly I feel like it gave me whiplash.

"Alex, can I call you that?" Trevor asks while inching closer and closer to me. I don't respond; something about this is making me want to run in the opposite direction and never look back.

"Uh, sure, but can you tell me why we're out here?" I finally responded after several seconds. A warm feeling enveloped me, and he wrapped his arms around me. My eyes start to twitch, and every signal in my body is telling me to run, as far as I can. But I don't, I stay there and let him. His warm lips meet mine, and I feel light as feathers. As if nothing in this world could pull us apart, ignoring how random this is, I kiss him more clearly wanting to stay here. Then, something sharp enters my mouth, I pull back, but his strong arms hold me in closer, I try pushing him and hitting him, but to no avail. I wake up in the dark, rocks beneath stabbing me in my back. I stand up, dusting the dirt off my body. I start looking around for an exit, but there isn't any light in here. I place my hands on the rough-textured walls.

"There are no doors," I cry out, a deep sob escapes my mouth, and the tears run down my cheeks and straight into my mouth. There are no doors, no windows, not even an echo from my own voice. "Where am I?"

It's the last thing I ever said.

KATHARINE KHO

[UNTITLED]

EAST BAY CENTER OF THE PERFORMING ARTS

I come from smokey streets
motorcycles and tuk-tuk's
Vendors trying to make ends meet
I come from a caring mother
A kind, understanding, and welcoming soul
Who came to the land of dreams
with nothing but her moral code
I come from keys and values
fifths, fourth, and thirds
I come from an orchestra, a band
A group of people who have the
ability to merge
They see me as loud,
They we me as being "too proud"
They try to push me down,
down, to make me want to frown
But I want
I'll continue to smile
Even if they hate crime me
5 times for every mile
My name is Katharine
With a k and an a nit an e or a c
Because I am a fighter,
a protestor
a leader
an activist
Someone who stands for what
she believes in, with a gift to
be able to resist, I am the people,
I am a democracy, I am the constitution,

I am nations, I am women, I am
a minority
And all these reasons are why I am proud to be me.

POEM

INGRID MOLINA ARELLANO

GIRLS INC. OF ALAMEDA COUNTY

On the Question of race

They ask me to write down my race
and I think and think very seriously
and consider writing down the truth
and have my answer read
I have the authentic Mexican food in me, that
gets erased with the American dinner we eat,
taco bell that isn't pure mexican. Growing up on
the side o'neill and sycamore street we have
la tienda chavez, and the ghetto jack in the
crack.
I have el olor a salsas y especias que envuelven
mi casa de pura tradición mexicana
I have the voices on accomplishing and
graduating high school.
I have the dream to became an engineer and be
able to give back to mi familia.
These are dreams yet to be accomplished
I grew up in a home where it's the hispanic
culture where men work and women clean.
The tradition that we reign and follow what our
parents say,
Or be left and sacrifice the consequences.
I have the memory of laying down while my
dignity is being taken from me
I breath to have my soul restored and heard
They ask me to write down my race
and I think and think very seriously
and consider writing down the truth
and have my answer read

I have the skin of non-mexican were i start to
wonder am i mexican
from house to house i grew with questions.
The strawberries, corn and cactus that grows on our
land
That was taken from us.
I went to Stonebrae, Bret harte, and mount eden
Do I fit in the standards now of a mexicano?

From hearing gunshots in the middle of the night
wondering could i be next
Having the self-doubt that I am doing enough
The McDonalds, pollo loco, that makes me envision
is this our future
from waiting at the bus stop to interacting with the bus driver
I think and say to myself, have I done enough
The ac transit, BART, southland mall, hayward police department
Written with words
"las malas acciones tienen consecuencias"
To the day i entered the world in the ghetto hospital st. rose
Is that who I identify as?
They ask me to write down my race
and I think and think very seriously
and consider writing down the truth
and have my answer read
My mom told me to never underestimate the power
and actions of a person
Times flies by us like the fastest animals on this planet
From conspiracies of aliens, and presidential elections
to the injustice served to the mexican communuity
Have they proved themselves that we are fit and
capable of fitting into society?
They ask me to write down my race
and I think and think very seriously
and consider writing down the truth
and have my answer read

I have los tamales en la noche y mañana de dias festivos
El atole de puro tamarindo y canale
end donde el presente trac recuerdos del pasado
Mis hermanas, mi madre, mis abuelos
Con el apoyo "se se puede"
To where they ask who I identify as
I say
Mexican-American

LYRIK HARRIS

"GROWING INTO ME"

EAST BAY CENTER FOR THE PERFORMING ARTS

I grew up strong, confident
I grew up knowing I could make it far
Knowing that there's a place for me in this vast, vast world
That no matter how hard it may be,
I can…
I can, right?
I grew up joyful, energetic
I grew up knowing I could be myself without putting on a mask
Knowing that I would be accepted for who I am, at least by my family
Wait…at least?
I grew up me, Lyrik, the name that holds a story, a song, a hope
The name that is an irreplaceable gift
A gift…
So why doesn't it always feel that way?
Why in the back of my mind, so I feel I'm not good enough?
That I, am not enough
Wait…pause
I <u>am</u> enough
I am strong, confident, joyful, energetic
I am me
And I am enough
I grew up knowing I'm enough
And no rejection,
No stereotype,
No curve ball that the world may throw at me will ever change that
Because I am me
I am Lyrik, not the name, but the girl
The girl that carries so much, a story, a song, a hope
Hope for the future
The future that I will grow into and claim as mine

POEM

KALIA GRIFFIN

ALBANY HIGH SCHOOL

Dance

all alone
spotlight on you
The music plays
And everything fades away
You flow
It's the utter peace of just letting your body move
Some moves fast
some slow
It all blends
levels
arms
legs
head
feet
all different movements
blending into one perfect movement
And it comes from pure instinct
Every part of your body
connects
moving
flowing
The lights fade
the music stops
You come back
out of breath
heart racing
feeling free
The music took over, and never be sorry it did

because it felt amazing
It felt like
freedom
grace
pride
Everything I'm not when the sun is out
When eyes are on me
But I am that when I have the music
the rhythm
the flow

FROM MT. MCKINLEY HIGH SCHOOL

CONTRA COSTA COUNTY JUVENILE HALL

2022–2024

AUTHORS IDENTIFIED BY INITIALS

2022

I want to go
home
B. G.

When I was born my mom was
incarcerated and I was in the
hospital all alone until my
grandmother came and pick
me up when it was my
time to go home to my
family because my mother
had to go back to
santa rita county jail
after she delivered me
and was ready to
be taken back to
her cell and think about
the newborn son
she just had
A. W.

Thug Emotions

You might be one of a kind but we all die the same
If you count to 100, would you still want to switch places?
Im going thru some thangs I pray its only phases
I seen niggas in they grave and I seen niggas get taken
I need a location shit getting shaky
I'm going in for all the ones I was raised with
Runtz in the wood Boi This shit so tasty
I only smoke cuz it take away the pain
Flashbacks in shootouts, high speeds,
we creep, kicking doors down
I guess I'm not somebody you can hold down
You told me that you love me
But you lied.
M. G.

When that gate is open
When these chains are broken
Do I get loaded
Or get a job and stay focused?
B. G.

I want to go
home
J. M.

2023

Do you hear me? I don't think you hear me
Poetry ain't for me, it ain't in me
But I try, and I'ma try
I ain't gone complain, and I won't change
I want to go home, but the judge actin'
Like she don't know
I ain't into writing songs, but my feelings are going far
As I sit thinking in my room wishing I

Was seeing the stars
I noticed that my actions weren't worth it
All along
After school I'ma go to sleep, when I
Awake I brush my teeth
I read book after book, it's boring and gets boringer
I pray they release me back to my father
I'm sad here, this place makes me mad
Why the police always take me away
When I start gettin' to a bag
D. A. C.

I'm physically caged but my mind is free
From sins. The evil is not in me
Why satisfy them? I got the key
Why give up hope when I could see
S. T.

When I hear success I think about power
A view where I can see the sun setting on the city
10 car garage filled with beamers and bentlys
My clothes fitted and my hair cut
My family straight
My friends straight
Everybody good
everybody around me got a purpose
everyone feel they worth
but naw let me get back to reality

the smell of metal
one wrong move the guards mad at me
doors closin
my buzzer goin off
dress code in order
they got me in a cage like I'm a dog
restless nights and cold days
jail food on rubber trays

you just wanna go back to sleep
back to my dream where I could fly away
M. C.

Red rose this
Red rose that
I'm the black one out the bunch
And that makes me *that* nigga
I. K.

A Letter to Hope
Dear hope,

Roses are red, violence is blue
My heart is dead; why aren't you?
I weep because I'm a monstrous creep
And when I sweep at you, you stay and don't decay

I must say, why do you stay?
Why don't you come at bay?
I guess you're here to stay

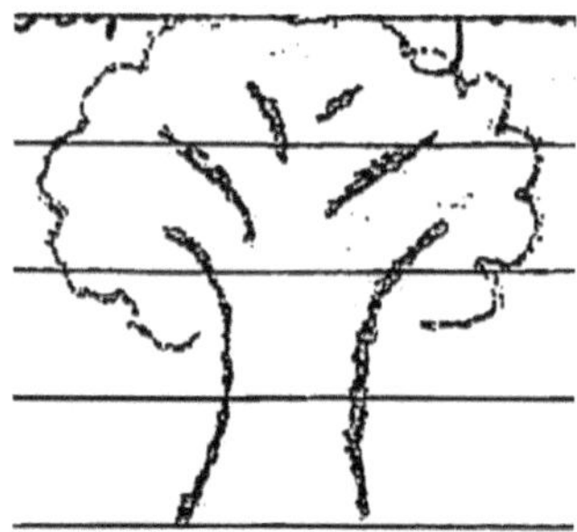

S. T.

You're growing up, you're not a little boy anymore
I feel as if it's time you figure it out some more
Jail is no home for you, stop thinking about others and
Think about you. Going down the right path will never
Go left again, spending more time with my family and my

Set of friends, you're so far away from home it feels
Like you won't make it back, you have support, and
You have goals, achieve them, be brave, be strong
And forever be positive, good things will come for all
My days that were cold, this road I'm stuck on isn't
Forever, but this is getting old. You promise you won't
Make mistakes know more, I know my choices were more
Than poor. Promise you won't make mistakes no more.
D. A. C.

When I think about freedom I think decisions,
the freedom to do what you want
When you want
The freedom to go where you want
Eat what you want
And see what you want
Freedom is the power to choose to be who you want to be around
To be who you want to be
To be free when you want to be free
M. C.

2024

Deep in a dream
Don't want to wake
But the light shines away
N. C.

The odds are stacked against you, they expectin' you to fail
But through the struggle and the hardships you still gotta prevail
You ask me how hard it is to find yo road to success?
It's like being in a haystack lookin' for a nail
You raised with a single mama
Family caught up in drama
Out there on yo own tryna run it yo and stack 'em
But you out there tryna do it all the easy way
And I'm here to let you know that ain't the only way

Expand yo mind and let God take the wheel
I promise you gone end up on top of that hill
N. T.

August, autumn
Leaves fall like a robe off a person
The trees are naked
N. T.

It is amazing
How when we are younger we don't think
We do immature things then we try to shrink

It is amazing
How I decided to go to school
Then started a fire like a fool

It is amazing
How I never thought about the consequences
Then I got expelled because of nonsense

It is amazing
N. C.

The hot sun
Insects crispy lying on the grass
The warm air going through my hair
C. P.

The whispering wind wound through the neighborhood
Blowing very softly, dancing through Maria's hair
And back out again, out into the open glare.
It rose, and fell again, like the belly of a snoring giant.
We need its breeze on a hot day, but it always likes to be defiant.
N. T.

You bother my soul
But I will eat you whole
To calm my soul
C. P.

We live & we learn
To strive & try to make it
Ms. U, Ms. Roxanne our guidance
N. T.

The waves are rushing
But still calm
The fishes fall for the bait
N. C.

Criddle the cat was calling for help out the tree. Teddy the cat came and climbed to help Criddle down, but became stuck himself. Teddy asked Criddle for help, but to prevent Criddle from getting stuck, told him to call others to assist. Criddle laughed and trotted away, happy to be out of the tree.
Moral: 1. Don't allow yourself to be used. 2. When you do something for someone, make sure they'll do it for you.
N. T.

There is light at the other side of the tunnel
Don't be impulsive and fumble
Just wait and earn everything you deserve
Just be patient and you will observe
Life is fine
You will shine
Don't forget the light at the end of the tunnel
Just hold your goals tight and strong
And you will not fumble

Trust me now you can do it
Now get to it and let's do it
N. C.

THREE POEMS

DAVID WOOD

For Alice—1949–2016

In her final days yes she did concede
To wear shoes, she who had trod barefoot
Through her gardens and along rocky paths,
Into airports and across continents,
Her shoeless walk for her as natural
As breathing. Now she wills that breath away,
Knowing her mind is no longer her own,
A tattered web that can no longer hold
Imagined worlds from which we weave a life.
Her aching hands and blurred sight stitched
Embroideries that hanging from our walls,
Each slow stitch a testament against time,
Speak now for her and for our lives sustained
And sweetened by their beauty, by their pain.

To Each Her Own

You do not know what beauty is she said
And bought the chest that held the old man's life.
Ugly I replied, and heavy as lead;
I wondered how sanity had left my wife
Here Look—those screws, these bolts, this corner piece—
To you random this collection might seem,
With each drawer I open my joys increase;
This handyman has built an artist's dream.
So squat it sits along our basement wall,
Dripping unknown treasures dressed in rust
These contents when seen anew can enthrall
An artist's eye that I have come to trust.
That chest whose entrance I would still refuse
Is serving now to spark my artist's muse.

Totems

She holds forked branches

And desiccated moss to the light

To see what it wants to be. Because she says

Nature breathes life

Even into dead things.

When it speaks it lives again, wrapped in string

And shadow.

A breeze sifts through the tendrils

Of its roots—ballerinas poised in shadow dance

Against the white walls of our imaginations

Shimmering on that sky beyond—

Past reason, past dreams that we humans know.

KEEP ON KEEPING ON

A STORY

RAYJON BRISCOE YOUNG

A summer breeze caressed the faces of a bunch of black boys and girls running in the street playing games–until the streetlights came on and painted their skin a fluorescent orange, stopping them in their tracks, signaling that the games had unfortunately come to an end. They all waved goodbye to each other, but this bye was different. Summer was over. It was Saturday night, yet they all knew they couldn't play again the next day. Some kids knew they had to go to church in the morning. Others knew they had last-minute back-to-school shopping to do. But Genesis just sat on the sidewalk. He waved bye to all his friends, wondering when they would all be able to play again.

Genesis thought about his friend Torian's barbecue from last week. All of his friends came out of their houses that day, and even the paleta man came by. His stomach grumbled a bit just thinking about it. Some guy from the corner store bought everyone an ice pop, too.

Genesis patted his pockets and found everything except what he was looking for. He got up, walked to his house, and fumbled through his pockets for the key. His hand grasped the doorknob, which was locked, and he figured his key must be inside. He went to sit back down on the concrete. He figured his mom would be home soon to let him in. Genesis pulls a book out of his lower pocket, using the streetlights to better see the pages.

The sidewalk rattled and rumbled as a baby blue Box Chevy rolled down the street. It looked vaguely familiar to him. It pulled up right in front of Genesis. He stood up, put his book in his cargo pocket, and began walking back to his house. He didn't know whose car that was and figured it wasn't there for him.

"Hey, youngin! You just gone walk away from me? I was gone ask what you was reading," the passerby yelled as he started to get out of the car.

"Who the heck are you?" Genesis turned around, stepping his right foot into the earth as if nothing could move him from the concrete, gripping his book tighter.

"Shit, my fault. I see you out here sometimes when I'm driving to the corner store. Some nights, for at least an hour after the lights come on. It's hard not to with those bright ass shirts you wear." Genesis, briefly glimpsing at his shirt, looked at the man with arched eyebrows and closed his lips, as though he was waiting for an answer.

"You not playing. My friends call me Deacon. Remember last week? I stopped by the barbecue and got y'all ice cream? Torian's parents made me a plate. Speaking of food. I was just about to go to In-N-Out. You like burgers? You want me to bring you one back? Unless you tryna to ride?" Deacon mimicked the face Genesis had just made.

Genesis brought his chin to his right shoulder to look at his house. He thought to himself that he should just stay there until his mom got home. But he didn't feel like waiting for his mom, she was probably going to come home late and fall asleep before cooking anything. Until the same breeze he had felt earlier pushed him forward a bit. Forcing him to take another step from where his feet were planted. At that moment, his stomach growled again, and he hopped in the car.

Deacon's car smelled like Little Trees Black Ice air freshener, cologne, and leather. The inside was so angular. The dashboard was a black and brown wood grain with all the bells and whistles, as if he had the car worked on.

"What's your name, youngin? My momma told me not to talk to strangers." Deacon fixed his rearview mirror before pulling off.

"You got jokes. Genesis. My friends call me Gen, though. This is a nice whip, Deacon. You do illegal stuff?" Genesis muttered as the car came to a stop. The bright red of the stoplight filled the car, and silence filled the air.

"Nah, I work for a security company. Shit I just got promoted last month, so I pimped my ride a lil' bit." Gen's eyes scanned Deacon; he had learned how to tell when adults were lying to him. The green light coated Deacon's face, and Gen figured he was telling the truth.

"How do you know Torian, Deacon?" Gen said, thinking about the barbecue.

"Me and his folks went to the same church. Torian and my son used to go to Bible study together." Deacon said while flashing his highbeams to get to the light to change.

"You go to church a lot?" Gen could see all of his religious tattoos, including a full sleeve with a big cross, angels, and clouds. It even had what he figured was a Bible verse.

"I used to. My father was a pastor. So my friends started calling me Deacon, and the nickname just stuck. Any more questions, Gen? Or can I focus on the road?" Deacon adjusted his hands on the wheel to turn into the car-filled drive-through.

"Yeah. Does God answer your prayers? I don't think he hears mine at all..." Gen paused for a moment to take a deep breath. "My mom comes home drunk sometimes. I guess she's still sad my dad passed away from sickle cell. I don't know my extended family that well. To take my mind off of things I end up reading..." Gen began to tell Deacon about his life, he didn't hold back either. That car turned into a face-to-face confessional.

"Damn. Do you need a meal or a therapist?" Deacon said after hearing Gen finished. "I'm just playing lil man."

"It's hella cars in front of us, so I'ma give it to you straight. I wouldn't say God answers my prayers, but he hears 'em. It's like six billion people on this rock. Shit we might not even be the only rock that got people on it. God got *a lot* of prayers to go through. You probably in line like we is now. Except you gone get this burger before he get to you. Plus, some things just beyond God's control. Wouldn't it go crazy if In-N-Out had a chicken sandwich? You nodding, but it's not gonna happen. God ain't gone change they menu. You feel me?" Deacon rolled his window down, wiped off his face, and sighed.

"Kinda. Dang, now I kinda want a chicken sandwich," Genesis's stomach growled even louder.

"Well, this Double-Double meal's gonna get you right. I promise," Deacon laughed.

As the taillights illuminated the line, the car inched closer and closer until the interior was filled with the aroma of grilled onions, french fries, and burgers. Deacon told Genesis he could eat in the car if he didn't spill anything on his new seats.

When they returned to Genesis's house, the lights were on. Deacon glanced at the house and then looked at him. Gen loosened up when he got the food, but became tense as soon as he saw the living room lights.

Deacon reached into his pocket, pulled out a folded stack of cash, and grabbed a few twenty-dollar bills. "Hold onto this. Get yourself a new book or something. Don't keep your mom waiting now."

Genesis opened the car door and dragged himself onto the sidewalk. He started walking towards his house, but turned around. "Deacon, what do you do when you feel like giving up?"

"Just keep on keeping on. It seems hard now, but it'll get easier." Deacon's phone started ringing, and he got back into his car. Genesis began walking up the stairs with his chin touching his chest. "I'll see you around, Gen! Keep your head up!"

He opened the door to his mom sleeping on the couch. She sometimes forgot to lock the door after a long day at work. Genesis sighed with relief, went to the hallway closet to grab a blanket, and covered his mom with it. He went to the snack closet and set a bottle of water next to her, too, since she smelled like she had made a stop at a bar before coming home.

That talk with Deacon reminded Gen about talks with his dad. The ones about random stuff. But this talk was the kind of talk that keeps your head on straight.

Gen overheard his mom get up and go to her room, and he saw the glow from her phone flashlight pass by under the door. She called one of her friends and told her that it was the last time she'd be going out after work like that. After hanging up, she groaned about not knowing where her son was, but figured he had gone to one of his friends' houses, as he usually did. He looked at his calendar and realized that this was the month his dad died. He heard his mom walk to the corner of her room where her dad's portrait was hung up, "I gotta turn it around now," she whispered before he heard her body hit the bed in exhaustion.

As he reached the last page of his sci-fi book, Genesis knew precisely what he would do with the money he had been given. He would save it for the Scholastic book fair his school would have in the first week of school.

It was Wednesday, and his school held a book fair in the library, allowing every kid to visit during lunchtime. After eating, he told his friends that he'd meet them on the black top after he hit up the book fair.

Thanks to Deacon, Gen had more than enough money to get what he wanted. So he got a nice illustrated chemistry book and a young adult novel, and he even had enough to get one more book.

"Damn, I knew I should've asked my dad for money the other day. I want this comic so bad," Gen overheard the kid next to him. He sized him up. The kid looked wildly familiar to him.

"Yo, I have some extra money left over, you need it?" Gen asked as he took the leftover money out of his pocket.

"Really? You're a good dude. Thanks, bro," he said.

"This isn't even my money anyway," Gen chuckled, "What's your name, bro? I feel like I met you somewhere before."

"My friends call me D. Maybe. You know Torian?" Gen nodded in response. "We used to kick it until I moved deeper in the west," D said.

The lunchtime bell rang, signaling that school was let out. Gen and D talked a bit about comics and books as they made their way outside. As D was getting picked up, he waved bye to Gen. As his hand returned to his side, he realized that he hadn't gotten to introduce himself.

—

It was the spring break of eighth grade, and Gen's mom went on a week-long cruise with his play auntie. He wanted to go, but his mom said she needed girl time. Gen knew he would get seasick, but just wanted an invite. His mom never shared some things with him, but deep down, he respected that. Lord knows he needed his alone time, too. With the house all to himself for a week, he decided to do nothing but read some new books, order takeout since his mom left him some money, and play video games until dawn. Sitting on his couch, he heard someone honk their horn twice outside. None of his friends had cars, so it must've been for somebody else. The car honked again, and he looked out the window. The hedges in front of his house block the street for the most part. So, he had to open the door to get a good look at who was honking.

He saw the cerulean blue box Chevy that decorated the block. That one commanded the most eyes out of every car on the street. With a new paint job that made the exterior look like liquid metal with shiny chrome accents. As if it were a spaceship.

"What took you so long? I already went to the store and came back." Deacon was floating down the block, throwing up peace signs to his friends loitering at the corner store. He still looked the same. Tall, and his hair always looked like it was freshly cut. You could always see the tank top under his shirt, as if he were born wearing it with his security work pants and some black steel-toe boots. The only thing that looked different about him was that he had half a dime's worth of left ear missing.

"You on spring break now, right? You was reading, huh? My fault," Deacon said while sizing Gen up. Gen had gotten taller. They were almost the same size, although Gen was skinnier. "Lock up and let's grab a bite, man."

Gen walked up to his house, went inside to grab his keys, and locked up. "I haven't seen you in a minute. How'd you know it was me?"

"Well shit I ain't stupid. Plus you still wearing them bright ass shirts. What color is that? Lavender?"

"I ain't fresh?" Gen stuck his arms and legs out as if he were mimicking the shape of a star. He wore brand new Air Force Ones and Girbaud jeans with a purple stripe. With a cropped lavender shirt to bring the outfit together.

"You fresh. Your swag's a lil different, that's all." Deacon says as they both get in the car.

Genesis got in the passenger seat, but this time it felt different. He sank into it a bit more than usual. They began to drive without a destination and ended up at Lake Merritt. They pulled into Anh's. Almost every time they got together, even if it was only a few times a year, they went to get burgers. A simple meal you can eat on the go and still have room for conversation. "I just got me a PlayStation 4, so we can get on that game you been bugging me about," Deacon says while dipping his fries in ketchup.

"Fasho! Text me your Gamertag, and I'll add you later tonight," Gen replied with a mouthful of cheeseburger.

"You about to graduate middle school soon, right? Where you going to high school at?"

"Head Royce! You know that preppy school in the cut by that temple on the hill?" Deacon nodded. "I got a scholarship," Deacon mouthed the words my man with a smile glued to his face. "I got it all mapped out, Deacon. I'ma go there, then get scholly from Cal and study Chemistry.

To keep it a hundred with you I don't think I would've gotten interested in Chem if not for this crazy book I got at the book fair with the money you gave me." Deacon looked so full of joy.

"Gone head then!" Deacon's phone started ringing, and he stepped out of the car and said he'd be right back. Gen was curious. He knew enough about Deacon, but not a lot; he was just a kind man.

"Sasha, you already got custody, and that's cool, but if he wants to see me, you gotta let 'em. He's about to go to high school, of course he wants to kick it with his dad more. Let me get the whole weekend, not just Sunday. Tell Deshé I'ma pick him up on Friday. Alright. I told you I don't care about all that. Let the boy like who he wants to like. Okay. I said alright. Love y'all," Deacon hung up the phone and walked back to the car. Genesis was on his phone, trying to look busy.

"Who took a bite outta yo ear man?" Gen pointed to his ear for reference.

"You got jokes. Nah, somebody shot at the client on a job, and it grazed me. You know how that shit go. Some of the rappers who have shows in the Bay also have enemies in the Bay. But at least the pay is higher on gigs like that. You got anywhere you need to be, or I can drop you back off in the west?"

Gen wanted to pry some more, but Deacon's leg started tapping, and whenever he did that, he had somewhere he needed to be. "I'm cool; I just got that new John Green book I wanted to finish today."

When Gen got dropped off, he threw a peace sign to Deacon and enjoyed the rest of his week of much-needed solitude.

—

It was the summer before undergraduate school, and Gen was sitting on the couch. "I'm so proud of you, baby." Gen's mom kissed him on his forehead. He was wearing his new Cal Berkeley shirt. He got up and went to the snack closet, looking for some water, bending over to feel around for the weight of the plastic container. But it was just empty plastic. The house phone started ringing, filling the room as he heard her run upstairs.

"Momma, I'm going to the store to get some water. Do you want anything?" Silence was followed by a faint no thank you as he opened the door.

Gen's graduation gift had arrived early, and he wanted to take the baby blue bike for a spin, but the store was only across the street. It smelled like it was going to rain, so he didn't want to risk it.

He waved to the fellas across the street, "Yo, when's the last time ya seen Deacon?" He had asked because it's been about two months since he was online and three months since he has seen him in person. The guys all shrugged as he went into the store.

"Y'all think we shoulda told Gen," he overheard as he checked out at the register. "Nah, it ain't on us to tell him. Maybe Sasha will reach out to him."

Gen ran out of the store and back to his house, full of a feeling he hadn't felt since he was a kid. To have someone randomly disappear and then learn they're dead. It reminded him of how his dad passed away. His mom didn't know how to describe it. His dad's side of the family got distant. No one talked to him about it. Enveloped with grief, he just sat on the sidewalk like he used to. The knot in his throat only got tighter and tighter. A breeze came down his block, blowing empty black plastic bags and cans.

The street rumbled, and when Gen heard that sound, he stood up fast and knew it could only be one person. To his surprise, he wasn't sure what to make of what he was seeing. It was Deacon's car, but it was dusty and dirty. A guy the same age as Gen hopped out of the vehicle holding a paper and his phone.

"You Genesis?" He nodded, his face filled with a distraught look.

"D?" He responded, confused and in disbelief. He was taken back to the middle school library for a brief moment.

"Yeah, man. Pleasure to finally know your name. You wanna sit in here, it's about to rain?"

"Dude, I never saw you again after I got you that book. Well, funnily enough, your dad got you that book." Gen said after he sat down.

"Yeah, bro, I had to change schools. My mom didn't want to use my dad's address anymore. Some petty shit to be honest. But hey, what can you do about it."

After what seemed like hours of conversation and getting to know each other, they realized they had shared so many similarities but had never met again after the book fair. They only heard about each other from Deacon.

"Yeah, I'm going to Cal, too. I'ma study Economics. I don't know what to do with it yet, but it seems interesting. I gotta go, though, my mom's blowing up my phone. She prolly mad I took the car without asking. I left my earrings in the glove box and couldn't find them shits for months bruh. Then I found a piece of paper next to 'em and ended up here." The rain taps make ambient sound, as though it were about to let up.

"One more question before you dip: why was he so nice to me?" Gen started tearing up. He remembered God had heard him.

"I don't know. I guess it was just because he was always kind... Maybe because he didn't see me enough and saw some of me in you," Deshé had put his hand on Gen's shoulder. The rain had finally stopped. Deshé and Genesis had exchanged contacts, bumped fists, and said their goodbyes. The car glistened as though the rain had washed away every impurity. Deshé stepped out of the car and waved goodbye to the person he had heard so much about, only to realize they had met before. For a brief moment, he looked just like Deacon. Gen wiped his eyes and went back inside. He was eager to start classes next week and hopes to see his new friend on campus.

"Let's get a burger sometime!" Deshé smiled brightly with that same smile.

"Fasho, I'd like that." Genesis smiled back at him.

POEM

ISA MALOOF

WHEN I HEARD THE NEWS ROE V WADE WAS STRUCK DOWN

I birthed him late in life. I knew I was not yet the person
I needed to be
to become a mother again.

Naked in the stream's music,
I, too, am simply tilting —
or, slipping—toward source

Which may also mean
living toward the confusion.
In this, some radiant choice.

RED, WHITE & BLUE

AN ESSAY

GENAY MARKHAM

When I saw the colors red, white, and blue in Kendrick Lamar's halftime Super Bowl performance in February 2025, during Black History Month, I could not help but think about what those colors mean to me. The performance served as a reminder that my ancestors helped build this great nation. Kendrick Lamar's dancers wore red, white, and blue. These colors were draped over black bodies while they moved gracefully across the stage to create different illusions using their bodies. As a painter, color is one of the ways I express myself. Color has impacted the way that I see the world. Color has impacted the way I see myself. Color has impacted my understanding of my identity and the legacy my ancestors have left me.

Red represents the blood of my ancestors that was spilled on American soil while they picked cotton, rice, sugar, tobacco, and indigo during slavery in the United States of America. Red represents the blood of Black people currently being murdered with the use of state-sanctioned violence. I am tired of being gaslit to believe the fact my problems as a Black person in America are just complaints. That I should "just be grateful" to be in the U.S., I can't tell you how many times I've heard the phrase "Slavery was so long ago," as if the intergenerational trauma caused by racism isn't still alive and well today. My response is but wasn't that long ago when two cops touched their guns as they stared at my brother, during an interrogation in the back room of his job, while accusing him of knowing a criminal they were looking for, instead of doing their jobs and committing resources to finding said criminal. It wasn't long ago that I was told by a white woman to get out of my seat so another white woman could sit down, in your oh-so-liberal San Francisco. It wasn't that long ago that a psychologist I was assigned to during a mental breakdown was telling me to go back to work even though I was too depressed to get out of bed, so how could I even make it to work? My body and mind weren't working. I did not feel like myself. I was not me. It wasn't that long ago that my mom was being harassed by white men at her job because she is the only Black female truck driver in her region.

The last couple of years of my life, I've tried so hard not to be political. But political is me. Politics is she. My ancestors' blood is the same blood that flows through me now. According to the hierarchy of race and gender in America, I am at the bottom, yet like cream, I rise to the top. Like a water spirit, I am resilient. That is what's beautiful about blood. And in some small way, through ancestry, our blood continues to flow like water through the veins, generation after generation. Adapting. Forming. Shaping. It's a link. It's a bond. It's a shared moment in time. The shared blood is a religion. The shared blood is a celebration. The blood we share with our ancestors is the reason we exist. Blood is creation, like billions of stars lighting up infinity. Blood is the soil from which humanity grows, like red draped on Black bodies.

White represents the spirit of our people. Because even when we weren't free, our spirits were always our protection. I am covered in this protection. Death is so common where I'm from in history. Even if our bodies can't be free, our minds are. How does someone survive hundreds of years of slavery? The spirit. Which is why it was the first part of humanity that was violated, tortured, and abused. Imprison your mind, and your body will follow. But our spirits aren't broken. Even if you ban diversity, equity, and inclusion, teaching Black history, or having Black History Month. Our country didn't even make Juneteenth a federal holiday until 2021, after the pandemic, after George Floyd was murdered by a cop in 2020, who knelt on his neck for 8 minutes and 46 seconds, while he yelled I can't breathe, and called for his dead mother because he knew he would be meeting her again soon.

I have been instructed to assimilate, to make my hair "neater," to be "submissive" and "quiet," and to be a "polite" lady. This is a slow chipping away of the spirit. Make my light duel. Turn me into a gray domino in a straight line with all the other pieces of the game we call survival. Spirit is something that hasn't died in hundreds of years. We dance in circles of white on the eve of a revolution which they will call a rebellion. When death is always near, be it a traffic stop, a knock at your front door, or an accusation, it makes your connection to the spirit closer because there has to be something better on the other side.

Blue represents liberty. We were liberated through water. We found liberty with access to oceans, bays, lakes, and rivers. There was running away, hiding in rivers from slave masters, jumping off of ships in the Atlantic, preferring sharks over bondage, or wading in water to keep the bloodhounds off our backs. Water helped my people to freedom in the North within the United States, and further north in Canada, once the slave catchers were legally allowed to start hunting us again. Water is like that of the life a mother carries, we give birth to our culture, for we are America too.

Blue represents the sky. My ancestors used astrology to get free. I remember reading the book, *Follow the Drinking Gourd* by Jeanette Winter, learning about the Big Dipper, Little Dipper, and that the star that shone the brightest was the North Star. The North Star was our trail to liberation in the sky.

Red and blue represent the gang's Bloods and Crips. Kendrick Lamar is from Compton, in Los Angeles, where these gangs reside. To see black bodies draped in these colors, dancing together, was a message of unity. Underneath the colors, all of the dancers were the same color, Black. Just like underneath our skin, we are the same color. It is a plea to look past what clothing is draped on the outside. It is an encouragement to focus on what we have in common as a people. I felt like Kendrick Lamar was saying we are all a part of black culture, whether you wear red or blue. Red and Blue are on opposite sides of the color spectrum, yet they danced together. Red and blue create the color purple. Purple is my favorite color.

These three colors, red, white, and blue, worn by black bodies, talented artists, and graceful dancers, were made into an American flag as a message to our nation, a statement, a declaration, a claim, and an inheritance that states, we too are America.

The football field was split into smaller stages and resembled a game of tic-tac-toe. Those nine boxes are like the boxes society tries to keep us in. Those boxes represent all the times someone told you to be, what to do, what you should look like, sound like, or act like, but all that does is limit you to one box. I think the tic-tac-toe imagery of the stage setup speaks to the idea that life is a game, and Kendrick is winning. White represents the spirit. His spirit can't be broken.

Serena, who is also from Compton, was doing the crip walk with a classy blue skirt and a royal blue jacket. The song "They Not Like Us" is about claiming our blackness, the West Coast as a region, and our nationality. Serena is not a Crip but she is from the same neighborhood where they reside. Crip walking is a way for her to pay homage to the soil, her birthplace, and her ancestry. It is a part of hip-hop culture to claim the soil that grew you. To protect and represent your region, your city, your place in the world. To be proud of where you are from is patriotic. Our ancestors fought so hard for us to have a place in the world that I understand this element of hip-hop. It is a simultaneous dance between geography, race, and nationality.

A hip-hop battle-winner is whoever does it better. The listeners of the music are the ones who determine the winner, not a corporation. It is a game like life. A game of skill. Hip-hop is also carrying on the oral tradition of storytelling that our ancestors used during slavery, when it was illegal for us to read and write. During those times, all we had were our minds and our memories. There's a spiritual connection to rhythm and rhyme, which also makes it easier to memorize things. Part of this history is the soil we stand on, these here United States of America.

"They Not Like Us" because they don't have the same struggle as us. "They Not Like Us" because we are Black. "They Not Like Us" because we're American. "They Not Like Us" because they don't understand how we speak. "They Not Like Us" because they don't understand the cultural significance of hip-hop. "The Not Like Us" because they (Aubrey, aka Drake) think it's funny to make jokes about slavery and wear blackface. Our history, Black history, is not a joke. It is a real lived experience.

"They Not Like Us" is an anthem for claiming all rights to name and protect our identity as Black people in America. An anthem similar to James Brown's, "Say It Loud – I'm Black and I'm Proud", except we are claiming ourselves by defining who we are not like. We are choosing not to assimilate after our language, customs, culture, and traditions were ripped away. Back when our existence was just a number or on a page, we claimed ourselves. As we always have. We claimed us when we celebrated Juneteenth back when no one else knew what it was. We claimed us by having black churches that kept track of lineages so that families who couldn't live together could be buried in the same cemetery and lie next to each other for an eternity. We claimed us by producing our own low-budget, black exploitation films that show blackness as everything: good, bad, evil, indifferent, beautiful, and a hero. We claimed us by celebrating black history week, which led to Black History Month, which will continue to be celebrated because to celebrate our survival is to celebrate life. Celebration is a testament to life, the breath, and the spirits within us.

TWO POEMS

GRACE DECKER

Tunnels

Driving down the roads I was only ever a passenger,
past wheat-colored hills and
littered meadows where deer still roam,
I hold my breath all the way through the tunnel and into the fog.

I am going to a house where nothing bears my name,
Where childhood simmers in corners without shame.

In the dream house that is neither a house nor a dream,
I am newborn and true.

The nasturtiums that bloom under redwoods and the stone river that cuts
through lady ferns and forget-me-nots spouted just yesterday

And the cathedrals
I built of untoward wishes and neglect turned inward are empty,
their stained-glass windows faded impossibly in time—
watch daylight pour out of my longing instead.

Here is the place where I finally let go of your hand. Here is where I find it.

In the dream house I am beckoned forward by a dragging past.

In the dream house I remember I am part of the world again,
that childish delights are still delights, and ready to be consecrated.

I listen to chickadees squabble and watch bumblebees live up to their names in the grass and leave them alone.
As a child I'd go out to the field during recess in the spring and lay my hands out in the grass in hopes that a bee would crawl into them. Often I'd get impatient and pick them up myself.

Before the sting I lauded my devotion, my understanding.

After I'd come up with an outlandish story of unavoidable danger, of victimless pursuit.
I'd just tripped and landed with an outstretched hand onto a bee. Or something flew into my hair, and when I went to brush it away I came back with a bee sting.

I thought everyone would fall for it. That other people could be a witness to the ways you fool yourself before you do felt cruel to me, even then.

To be the fool who can only wholly embrace in retrospect, to be the lab rat pressing the button for a shock and a morsel of food it knows is not on the other side, over and over, what else is there to do but cup your hands and wait for the sting?

Gone are the days I go to forget your name;
It's a stilted wonder, these native burnings all the same.

Autotomy

Been at my parents' house less and less this spring and the cat's retaliated by remembering his teeth.
That docile creature, who greets every potential intruder, whose reigning desire is to chew on dead grass, has begun to bite lizard's tails clean off to paw at what they leave behind, to leave dead mice at my door.

Their tails twitch in curled despair, the kind of mutilated reverie of the body that comes only after you've left it. Lizards can regrow their tails, sure, but it's a mix of cartilage, not bone. You will always be able to tell the point of rupture, of departure.

But the cat has no interest in lizards once their tails are gone. The allure of dead things that only beat out of habit pulls him from the rushing hearts in front of him.
Sometimes I'll come home to find one already inside, frozen in fear on the windowsill while the cat runs by, oblivious, to meet me at the door.

Today I found a bird, a sparrow, maybe, tucked into its side under the coffee table. Save for the cat hairs fixed in its beak and eyelids half-open, it could've been asleep. That's how peaceful it looked, how unscathed. The cat was nowhere to be found.

Outside in the breeze I became unconvinced of the fact of its death, for its feathers rippled so carefully in the sun and its talons bent and curled as I wrapped it in a towel. Carefully, I lifted its wing with a fingertip and touched its breast. That I had touched that soft and tender spot where its heart lay at all revealed its death in a way that the startling cold underneath the feathers wouldn't, because what thing precious and alive would ever allow a human so close?

I dug a shallow grave as deep as the brittle soil would allow and placed the sparrow in a box of my mother's anti-aging peptide eye cream and a dried rose cut from where I would be going. Covered the grave in river rocks to try and keep away the animals, but either way, I won't be there at night to hear the howling.

WHO NEEDS POETRY.

AN ESSAY

DREW KISER

Seven locked doors stand between the entrance to the Contra Costa County Juvenile Hall and the classrooms inside it. At every door you have to press a button and wait. Someone in a control room somewhere, watching my progress on CCTV, flips a switch to buzz me in. Even after a few months this remained a disquieting experience. More disquieting were the few instances where they unlocked the door before I pressed the button. Someone was watching me, anticipating my next move. I am a teacher with eyes on the back of his head: only, the eyes are not my own.

Every session of the poetry writing workshop I taught at Mt. Mckinley School at Juvenile Hall felt like standing in front of a locked door. Part of this challenge was the strangeness of the layout: I stood at the front of the class, with the permanent teacher sitting at her desk, and an armed security guard stationed in the corner. The students had incredibly demanding schedules, and our sessions were punctuated by people coming into the room to pull out students for counseling sessions, therapy, or meetings regarding their cases. Even when I taught college composition at San Quentin, the classroom was a relatively sacrosanct space, one which correctional officers would excuse themselves for breaching. The interruptions were a constant reminder of a system that considered ours an ersatz classroom, populated with kids who were students only incidentally.

The first lesson went smoothly. We talked about the differences between "aroma," "odor," "smell," and "fragrance." Which are natural and which are unnatural? Which colors do you associate with each? What are their tempos – which ones ask you to slow down and which require quick action? The students seemed unconvinced about poetry *per se*—but they were interested enough in this exercise about the quiet valences of connotation.

Before my second lesson, the teacher pulled me aside. At some point during the first lesson, I had told the students I pulled an example "out of my butt," a bowdlerization of a common expression. But the teacher warned, "Don't underestimate how homophobic people here are." It had not occurred to me that my butt, and the traffic in and out of it, would be a subject of interest for these students. My students at San Quentin, most of whom had been incarcerated since before *Will and Grace* (and at least one of whom before Stonewall) had never treated me or my "festive" identity with anything other than respect. Another door, locked.

But perhaps the biggest challenge was the student attitude toward, well, attitude. During a class on Haiku, a student requested that we learn material more relevant to their lives. He suggested rap. Though I was wary of becoming a backward-seated "cool teacher" stereotype that uses hip-hop to teach about Shakespeare, I brought in lyrics from Kendrik Lamar to discuss. We listened closely to the rhythm of his words, how he played with emphasis and rhyme to create satisfying arrangements. It was a good class. Though at the end, the same student informed me that "no one listens to Kendrick anymore." Rather than argue, the next class I brought in a sample of this student's favorite rapper, J. Cole. We traced Cole's use of stressed and unstressed syllables to discern the pattern he was working with, then explored how he wove end rhyme, consonance, and assonance into an aural tapestry. We marked up the verse with different colored markers. "But J. Cole doesn't think like that," objected the student. "He's a freestyler. He doesn't even write his lyrics down." The next class I brought in a snippet from an interview with J. Cole where he talks about how he writes all his lyrics down. In fact, Cole shares, he does write his two Artist's Way pages every morning. I showed this interview to the class, interested to see how that one student would respond. "I don't believe that," he said.

I felt like I was standing in front of a locked door, ringing a bell that no one was listening to. When students are sulky or bratty, my impulse is to yield nothing, to remind them that the work we're doing here is important. But these students live in a constant state of denial. This was a residential unit where even bringing in Rice Krispy treats was considered so indulgent that it required a request to the administration months in advance. (We never did get the Rice Krispy green-light.) The walls these students erected between me and them was a form of self-protection in an unfeeling carceral system. Was my determination to break through these doors just another violation?

In the last class, though, something happened. We were talking about slant rhymes, and I asked them if they knew why no words in English rhyme with "orange." It has to do, I said, with its unique history. "It comes from Sanskrit originally, then through the Middle East?"

My teacher, whose first language was Urdu, told us that in her language orange was "nārangī." The security guard, who spoke Farsi, said in that language it was the similar "naranji."

"Does anyone know what 'orange' is in Spanish?"

A student whose first language was Spanish replied, "naranja."

"That's how it was when it first came to Europe. As the word traveled north from Spain and Italy, the aspirated 'j' sound transformed into a harder 'g.' So if you showed a guy in Medieval England an orange, he would say, 'that's a narange."

I turned to the class. Could they anticipate what happened next? The excitement must have been clear in my face: for the first time all semester, every student was paying attention.

"Then the 'n' shifted over. 'A narange' became 'an arange,' then 'an orange.'" I showed them how this happened to a few other English words, a terminal or beginning "n" flipping from one word to the next—napron becoming apron, ewt becoming newt. "It's called misdivision," I said, to a class agog.

I wanted to shout: this is merely one knot in the gorgeous net of language! Our world is enmeshed in a linguistic pedigree that simultaneously binds and capacitates our imagination! At a unit as small as a word, they understood. But when I showed them how these pedigrees manifest in poetry, the doors swung shut again. I finished the session and left. And I'm not entirely sure what, if anything, I managed to teach them.

There's a sticker on the wall of the cubicle I share with two other literature grad students that reads, "Who needs poetry." Period and all. A question mark would have made this phrase brazen – who needs poetry, it would imply, when there are so many more consequential needs? If Maslow were to put poetry anywhere on his pyramid, it would have been perched on the tippy top like the multicolor propeller on a toddler's hat. But the period at the end turns this into an adjectival phrase, an appositive to a phantom subject who, in its totalizing absence, is all of us. Or perhaps it's more specifically "the student," as in "this is the student who needs poetry." To understand the fabric of language that swaddles us all, to open locked doors, to understand why some words are so resistant to rhyme.

PART THREE

DEMOLITION

A STORY

FIONA McFARLANE

"The Biga house is coming down," Gerald said. "Finally." He took the tray from Eva's lap.

"That lovely house," Eva said.

Gerald held the tray in one hand and, with a finger of the other, lifted a slat of the venetian blinds. He peered out the window. "What's lovely about it?" he asked, and the tray tilted.

"Gerald!" Eva called, and he righted the tray without looking at her. "The Japanese maple with the crimson leaves."

"They dug it up already," Gerald said. "Worth a fortune, a tree like that."

Eva wheeled herself to the window.

"I'll open the blinds," Gerald said, but he went away first, into the kitchen with the tray. Until he came back, she studied the dust on the edges of the blinds—the very thin rim of it. But who could fault Gerald, who was tremendous with the housework and had said, "What's wrong with curtains? Blinds'll only catch the dust," and still let her have them installed? Now he came back and leaned over the couch the way you had to and fiddled with the cords of the blinds until Eva could see the Biga house.

"So many cars," she said, and Gerald snorted.

A man approached the Biga house and stopped at the front gate. He said something to the workmen inside the fence, and, when they answered him, he turned to the letter box—an ordinary metal letter box—and, with one sure movement, wrenched it off its post. Then he cradled it against his stomach the way you might a heavy watermelon and carried it to a car parked down the street.

"Souvenir," Gerald said. "Sickos."

But he stayed at the window to watch for the excavator. When it came around the corner, the doors of the cars parked on the street all opened up, and people rose out of them. They held cameras and camcorders, and they wore clothes in muted colors—like the ones you see on TV journalists in war zones, Eva thought. As if they wanted to hide themselves. And all there to watch that little house come down. Eva had been a girl inside that house, visiting the Laineys. And after the Laineys moved to Sydney, she had seen tenants come and go, the shutters loosen and tighten, the maple tree's red turn on and off each year. Some tenants had raked the leaves, and others hadn't. Some of her students had lived there with their families, and there had been nights when the windows were lit and music came out of them, and fatty smoke from grilling lamb chops. Christmas trees in the front window. So many women standing at the gate, calling children's names. And sometimes pets—the Bigas themselves had had a dog, and later Paul Biga had all those birds. All of that, today, would go.

The street was getting crowded now. Workers in hard hats called out for people to stay back, and along came Jim Grant, who still looked, in his police uniform, like a big, red-cheeked tenth grader. Behind him was a woman Eva thought she knew, a short woman in a navy suit, who seemed almost superstitiously not to look toward the Biga house—and, yes, it was their house, Eva and Gerald's, that she was looking at, their gate she opened, their path she stepped onto.

"Who's this, then?" Gerald said. He liked to get to the door before a visitor. He was so large he filled the entire doorway—Eva knew how wonderful it was to see him waiting there, with his big voice calling "Welcome!," and how imposing he was if the welcome didn't come. She went back across the room to her usual place and listened to him say hello, and he was gracious as he said it; his tone was affable. So he approved of the short woman, and would admit her.

"You've got a visitor," he said, coming back in from the hallway.

The woman was the type who put her head around the door before she entered a room: here was her head, light hair, sharp nose, and now here was her body. Was it to conceal her shortness? Eva understood these strategies; she didn't like people to see her wheelchair before they saw her face.

"Hello, Mrs. Forsythe," the woman said, bending to kiss Eva's cheek, perhaps because Eva had lifted her face.

"This is a Miss Kate Hawkins," Gerald said. "Says you're old mates."

"Oh, no!" the woman said. She wore a bag across her body—it flattened one breast. "I mean—I wonder if you remember me?"

"One of your old students, love?" Gerald said.

But Eva knew now who she was: she was the woman who'd written the book about Paul Biga. Her hair was lighter, but otherwise she looked the same. Eva nodded

"I might pop out," Gerald said. "If you ladies are all right? See how old Terry's getting on."

Eva could imagine Terry—next-door-neighbor Terry, with whom Gerald was at war but only on Monday evening, garbage night—was standing on his lawn to watch the Biga house come down. So Gerald went and joined him, and Eva knew exactly how they would look: Gerald Forsythe and Terry Jarrett, feet planted firmly, arms crossed high on their chests, as if they were supervising the demolition. Which could now proceed.

The short woman said, "Perhaps you don't remember, Mrs. Forsythe. We spoke some years ago, here in this room, about Paul Biga."

"Yes, I remember," Eva said. "But was that really five years ago?"

"It was 1998. October. Just after the federal election."

"Well, goodness, years!" Eva said.

"I was writing a book. Did you ever receive a copy? I gave the publisher your address."

"You know, I think we did." Eva gestured at the bookshelf.

Kate Hawkins walked towards it, and there, as if by magic, was the book. Kate pulled it off the shelf and handed it to Eva: a black jacket, red letters, and that lurid title. *Hunter on the Highway: The True Story of a Monster Among Us*. The cover was a closeup of Paul's adult face, most of it in shadow, except for the bland blue of his eyes.

Kate Hawkins said, "It's all right if you never read it. I wouldn't blame you." She seemed uncertain, standing there in stripes of light—the blinds—with the Biga house behind her. "And now I'm working on an article—five years later, looking back, and the house coming down.

How have people coped? How has the town changed? Or not? Where are we now? That type of thing. Because it was all so raw back then."

Eva remembered, now, how much this woman had talked at first—how tentative it made her seem, how apologetic, until, in putting her at ease, you found that you had talked too much yourself. Eva recognized this trick because she'd used it many times—not so much on her students as on their parents.

"How about some tea?" Eva said, moving toward the kitchen so that Kate Hawkins couldn't ask or make some gesture that would mean "Can you manage?" or "Let me do that for you." Eva was handy in the kitchen; she could make a pot of tea and set some biscuits on a plate. Gerald put everything she needed in the lower cupboards.

"What have you been up to since I saw you last?" Eva asked, deliberately chatty among the mugs and tea bags.

"Oh, this and that," Kate Hawkins said. "A lot of articles, another book."

"More murders?" Still in her brisk, deliberately oblivious voice.

"Yes, a matricide," Kate said, quite casual, and then, "It's shocking, really, that murder pays my bills."

"I wouldn't say 'shocking.' Could you carry the tray, dear?"

Kate Hawkins, with the tray, followed Eva back into the lounge room. She set the tray on the coffee table and perched on the edge of the couch, exactly as she had five years ago. "What I wanted first of all," she said, "was to apologize for coming so soon after Paul's arrest."

"You did come rather swiftly," Eva said.

"It had to be the first book out—payment was double if I was first."

"And was it quite a lot?"

"It was," Kate said. She didn't, now, seem ashamed. "Down payment on a house."

"Good," Eva said. And it *was* good—to turn a murderer into a house. What a clever thing. She picked up Kate's book, with Paul's face on it.

Kate blew at the steam above her tea. "Journalists get so used to barging in. To be perfectly honest, I saw you simply as an opportunity—neighbor, school principal, employer. Your garden's looking lovely, by the way."

“That’s all Gerald, now that he’s retired,” Eva said. “No need to pay anyone to do it for us.”

“I wanted to say—I wanted to apologize, but also to say what an impression you made on me when we spoke, Mrs. Forsythe.”

“You must call me Eva. You did before.”

“Thank you. Perhaps you won’t remember, but I asked if you had children and you said no. A few minutes later, you wanted to change your answer. Do you remember?”

Eva shook her head. What had she said to anybody, years ago?

“You said, ‘I was a teacher and a principal. That’s how I had my children.’”

“Oh, yes,” Eva said. She’d made this statement a number of times, to different people. Maybe it had seemed clever at first, or deeply felt, or simply dutiful—it didn’t surprise her to hear that she’d said it to this journalist.

“I wanted you to know how much that moved me,” Kate Hawkins said. “I think of it often. My daughter is in second grade.”

Eva was reminded, then, that Kate had asked a lot of questions about Paul’s mother. That was why she’d waned to know if Eva had children: it was a way into asking about Lucinda Biga. And Eva thought, at the time, how unfair it was that mothers are so often blamed for their children’s sins.

A fearsome noise began outside.

“Goodness, what a racket,” Eva said. She noticed that she was rubbing her thumb against Paul’s shiny face on the book jacket.

Kate glanced at the window. “You’re not interested in watching?” she asked.

Eva took a sip of her tea. “I’m not the one writing an article,” she said. Shouldn’t you be watching?”

Kate Hawkins laughed. “I have someone outside recording it. I’d much rather talk to you. What does it mean to you that the Biga house is finally being demolished?”

“Are we onto the official interview now?”

Kate laughed again. “May I record our conversation?” She produced a Dictaphone from her bag.

Gerald would disapprove of this, just as he'd disapproved of *Hunter on the Highway* and of all the people who had come to gawk, even years after Paul's arrest, at the Biga house; who'd taken photos and plant cuttings, who'd knocked on doors, who'd left tributes to the people he'd killed, and who'd parked badly in the street. Gerald would have had the Biga house demolished just to get some peace; he'd threatened, once, to set it on fire, and been annoyed with her for crying as if he'd meant it. Gerald had called her sentimental, but Eva didn't think she was. Maybe she would feel differently if Paul had brought his victims to the house; and maybe she wouldn't. There was something in that house, quite aside from Paul, that should persist.

"Yes," Eva said. "You can record. What was the question?"

"How do you feel about the Biga house being demolished?"

Eva placed *Hunter on the Highway* face down on the coffee table beside her mug of tea. There was a photo of Kate on the back, looking approachably pretty in a pastel shirt.

"Well, first of all," Eva said, "it isn't the Biga house. It's the Lainey house."

"Lainey?"

"The Lainey family. L-a-i-n-e-y. Mr. Lainey built it in the early twenties, a year or so before my father built this place. They've rented it out for years and years—since, let me think, 1946. Yes, I was sixteen when they left. The Bigas came in the late seventies. They were the Laineys' longest tenants—more than twenty years."

"They moved to Barrow in 1976," Kate said. "And Biga's father moved out in early 1999, a few months after the arrest."

Eva supposed this must be right. "You know," she said, "this isn't a tenant kind of town. It's a town where people die and then their children live in their houses. So people were funny about that house, about everyone who lived there, though by the end most people forgot that the Bigas didn't own. They took good care of it, the Lainey house."

Maybe no one else in town still referred to it as the Lainey house; Gerald certainly didn't. But when Jan Biga and his wife, Lucinda, and their teenage son, Paul, had moved in, it was to the Lainey house. "I hear there's a Pole moved in to the Laineys'," Gerald said, and Eva thought at first he meant a pole, a post. He meant, of course, a Polish man.

How literal she was about the Lainey house. It was as if she couldn't absorb the changes that had taken place there: the Laineys leaving, Josie Lainey waving goodbye from the back window of their car; the tenants moving in and out; the Japanese maple turning its intricate red; the Bigas arriving, and teen-age Paul crossing the road to work in the Forsythes' garden for seven dollars an hour. Last time Kate Hawkins had come, just after Paul's arrest, she'd asked about those gardening days. Had Eva ever noticed anything unusual about him—anything that might have given an indication of the monster he turned out to be? "Oh, no," Eva had said, a quiet boy, and so polite you'd never dream—that kind of thing. She remembered later that when Paul had come to do the garden the first time, she'd noticed the length of his fingernails. He used to pinch caterpillars out of the gardenias with those long nails. Was that a sign of anything? But Paul was only ever a sign of himself.

"It's hard to think of it as a family home," Kate said.

"Not for me," Eva said.

Mrs. Lainey at the gate calling, "Josie! Josie!," her hands caught up in her apron; ham on the Lainey table; hands swatting at flies all through the saying of grace, the laziness of lunchtime flies, the slowness of hands during grace, and Josie's foot pressing Eva's under the table; the organ in the front room with its odd, resisting pedals, Mr. Lainey playing it with a bottle of beer beside him on the stool and Josie turning the pages of the music; Eva holding the baby while Mrs. Lainey hung the washing, white drool staining Eva's arm and her never minding, Josie sulking at how much Eva loved the baby; Josie asking, "Would you save Harry Cox if his house was on fire? Would you save Norman Monk?," running through all the boys in their class, "Would you save John McInnes, Gerald Forsythe? Would you save Michael Byrne?"; Josie walking the brick fence wearing a yellow dress and red lipstick; Josie, Josie, Josie.

Kate waited for a particularly loud burst of noise to pass. Then she said, "And how do the Laineys feel about having had Paul Biga as a tenant? Do you know?"

Josie Lainey throwing a cricket ball at her brother, missing, laughing, dodging when he threw it back.

"No idea," Eva said. "We lost touch. I can't imagine they like it. Of course, Mr. and Mrs. Lainey were gone well before—well, everything."

"When did they pass?"

Eva disliked the euphemistic use of "pass," especially from a woman who earned a lot of money describing death in vivid detail. She said, "They died in the early eighties, I believe."

Mrs. Lainey and Josie sitting on the stuffy sofa in the front room—the formal room, which no one ever used. They were holding hands, their faces pale. Mr. Lainey guiding Eva into the hallway, saying, "All right, Evelyn, you'd better go on home now," and closing the door very softly.

Eva left in the hallway, sobbing without making any sound.

Kate Hawkins asked, "How many children in the Lainey family?"

"Three."

"Their names?"

Josephine, Michael, Margaret.

"Oh," Eva said, "I wouldn't be comfortable. They won't want their names associated."

"I understand," Kate said, and wrote a few words in her notebook.

I suppose, Eva thought, she'll simply look it up or ask someone else. If she were my student, I'd want her to be canny and resourceful; I'd insist that she go on until she'd found her answers.

Kate took a sip of her tea. "So, they built the house in the early twenties, and they left in—did you say 1946? Just after the war. They'd lived there for at least twenty years. Why did they move?"

There had never been a face, or lips, or arms more beautiful to Eva than Josie Lainey's. Not even Gerald, whom she had loved and desired for years, had ever lain like Josie in a bed, as if there were no clear distinction between her body and the warmth, the softness, the sweetness of the sheets.

"Mr. Lainey got a job in Sydney."

"What kind of work did he do?"

The front door opened and the noise of the demolition increased, then was muffled again. Gerald arrived in the lounge room, rubbing his hands.

"Just getting my camera," he said. "Might take a photo or two," he said.

"Is it already down?" Eva asked.

"Front rooms are down," Gerald said, hurrying through to his study. "Bedrooms to go. They certainly know how to get the job done, once they've put their minds to it."

Josie Lainey's bedroom, done all in pink (Josie eventually too old for this, rolling her eyes, not a baby anymore), had become Paul's. And Eva wondered, sometimes, if there had been some residue left in that room, some trace of Eva and Josie. It wasn't the kind of thing she ordinarily considered. But it would be one way to explain, wouldn't it, the letter Paul had sent?

"Are you tired, Eva?" Kate asked. Her face was creased with concern; Eva didn't trust it.

"Not at all," Eva said. But she was tired. "What was your last question?"

"What kind of job did Mr. Lainey move to Sydney for?"

Gerald erupted from his study carrying his chunky camera. "He didn't move for a job, did he?" he said. "Wasn't it some kind of family drama? That's what I heard. They certainly left pretty quick smart."

"A drama?" Kate said, sitting up straighter on the edge of the couch.

"It was definitely a job," Eva said. "He worked in agricultural machinery. He'd been a salesman, and he was promoted to a larger district."

Gerald shrugged. "Evie would know," he said, then launched into the hallway and out the front door. The sound of the demolition rose with the opened door, then receded again.

"You were close to the Laineys?" Kate asked.

Eva said, "The older daughter was in my class at school."

"The same school you went on to become principal of?"

"The high school, yes, but we started kindergarten together."

"The same school Paul Biga attended," Kate said.

"The high school, yes," Eva said. "Eventually."

"Paul was at the school for years ten, eleven, and twelve," Kate said, and Eva nodded. "Did you often hire your students to work for you?"

Eva looked at the photo of Kate on the back of *Hunter on the Highway*. Her chin was resting on her left hand, and she wore a wedding ring. She wasn't wearing one now. Eva had only skimmed the book, looking for any mention of her name or Gerald's. She'd seen snatches here and there—

Paul's "prowling taxi" and "the sinister underbelly of Barrrow's storybook appeal and "the mute silence of his victims, known and unknown"—before finally finding herself. She occupied three sentence, in which the implication was that she, in her provincial naïveté, had been hoodwinked by Paul's calculated charm. To live living opposite a monster without recognizing his evil might, Eva supposed, require a special variety of delusion. Others in town had been quick to say that there was always something off about him.

"My students? No," Eva said. "We hired Paul as a neighbor, more than as a student. A neighborhood boy."

"He was seventeen when he started," Kate said, as if riffling through mental files. "And he came every day?"

"I thought we were talking about the Lainey house," Eva said. She wanted Gerald to come back now, to fill the door frame, to recognize her distress and drive the woman away from the house with his forceful conviviality.

"We are," Kate said. "Did Paul work in his parents' garden, too?"

"He spent a lot of time out at the aviary," Eva said. "The Laineys built the aviary."

Josie with a cockatoo on her head, the cockatoo screaming, "Give us a kiss! Give us a kiss!"

"The Laineys kept birds?"

"Yes. A sulfur-crested cockatoo."

"Just the one? Did they take it with them when they moved to Sydney?"

"No," Eva said. "They set it free. It lived in the garden for months, then eventually it was gone."

"And did any of the other tenants keep birds in the aviary?"

"No," Eva said. "Only Paul."

Paul bringing her, shyly, a glossy offering of magpie feathers; Eva saying, "Oh, my mother would have used these to trim a hat," and then not knowing what to do with them, so they lived in a mug beside the telephone for more than a year. Black-and-white pennants.

"It was still in good shape, then?" Kate asked. "The aviary? If the Bigas came in seventy-six, the aviary hadn't been used for nearly thirty years."

"Paul repaired it," Eva said. Gerald had helped him. Gerald had always been handy. He'd wanted children.

"So, gardening at your house, but birds at home," Kate said. "Did he come every day?"

"We couldn't have afforded for him to come every day."

"Your neighbors," Kate said, "on this side"—she pointed in the direction of the Jarrett house, Terry Jarrett of the sloppy garbage bins—"remember him coming nearly every day."

Well, yes, there had been those few weeks one summer when he came most days, without asking for extra payment. You would look out a window and see him deadheading the daisies, or you'd hear a sound and it would be Paul sweeping the front path. If you opened the door and offered him a cup of tea, he always said no. There was only one task he refused, and that was killing stinkbugs. It was Eva who had picked the stinkbugs off the kumquats by hand and dropped them in a jar of methylated spirits. Gerald had offered to spray, but she didn't want chemicals on the fruit trees, and Paul was too disgusted to touch the stinkbugs, even with gloves on (Paul, who would allow spiders on his bare palms and throw snails hard against the fence to crack their shells and keep them out of her irises). But Eva had been fascinated, had noted the frantic waving of the stinkbugs' striped antennae, had made herself dizzy with the fumes of metho and stink that rose from the jar, had watched as valiant bugs pulled themselves to apparent safety on rafts made of other bugs until she tilted the jar, creating terrible tsunamis. The jar was full of clinging death and gave her great satisfaction. The kumquat tree, no longer under attack, had put forth fruit and blossom and been visited by bees; the marmalade Gerald made from it (an excellent maker of jams, Gerald) was delicious spread on toast or on thick slices of cheddar cheese. She had dumped the bodies of the bugs in one corner of the garden and, after the alcohol evaporated, the ants had made feasts of the softer flesh.

"He came three hours a week," Eva said. "Usually on Saturday mornings. That's what we paid him for. But haven't I already told you everything I can about Paul? I didn't know him well, especially once he finished school. The Bigas moved in their own circle."

By which Eva meant they had kept to themselves. Jan Biga was invariably polite, but there had been a chill to it, a sort of distrustful reserve, as if his ramrod posture and faultless manners advertised how little he wanted you to know his business. He never took to Gerald; but then, Gerald neve made much effort with him.

"Their own circle," Kate said. "Of course. But living across the road—" She gestured towards the window.

Eva imagined a yellow machine clambering over the that used to be the front room of the Lainey house. The windows in that room had been set with squares of stained glass; she and Josie used to find it funny, in the afternoons, to lie on the floor so that the squares of blue and red light fell on their chests, exactly where their breasts would one day be. The tender pucker of Josie's breasts. Looking back on that last year with Josie—1945 and into 1946—Eva marvelled at how chaste they'd been, how pure. Even their kisses, full of heat, had been wholesome. The stained-glass windows had been removed before the demolition. By whom? Eva wondered.

What Kate meant, of course, was that you learn things about people when you live so close to them, even if you don't spend time together. That you notice things without meaning to—surely you notice things. Nobody wanted to believe Eva when she said that Paul Biga had seemed like a perfectly ordinary boy. And he had, although one of the things Eva had learned as a teacher and a principal was that there are no perfectly ordinary adolescents, that each of them is strange, and bewildered, and in mourning, because they're all in exile from their childhoods, just as they always longed to be. There had been only one thing that marked Paul Biga as unusual, and Eva had never told it to anyone—not even Gerald. At the end of that summer when he'd come to the garden every day, Paul had written Eva a letter on those thin sheets of paper—so thin that if your hands were even a little damp the paper became translucent or tore, the paper that people used when they were sending letters overseas and wanted to keep the weight down. The things he said he'd planned for them: a farm, and horses, an aviary, of course, and, because he knew she loved the maple tree in his front garden, he would dig it up to bring with them, he would plant it outside their bedroom window and every night he would, and she would, and then he would, and would, and would—How detailed he was—her pussy, her arse, her tits—how well he spelled when he spelled her body out, and how lonely that seemed, to spell "cunnilingus" right and "specific" wrong. In what film, what TV show had he seen the farm with the gentle, sexual, older wife, or learned about love letters, so that he could approximate one now, for her? And what was the sign he'd wanted her to give him? A candle in the window, or something just as ludicrous—as if Gerald wouldn't have noticed a candle! As if a candle in the window wouldn't catch the curtains on fire and burn down the house, as if someone walking along the street wouldn't see a candle in the Forsythe window with the lights all off and think, I'd better knock on the door. They've gone to bed with a candle burning. And the terror, then, lying in bed, that he would come anyway, would be a candle himself waiting at the door, coming into the house, standing over her in the bedroom. Would you save Eva Forsythe if her house was on fire?

She could have told someone, told Gerald or spoken to Paul or to his father, but she hadn't. Which had probably been irresponsible of her, but Paul had just graduated from school, his mother was very ill with the cancer that went on to kill her, and the letter was so passionate, so precise, that she worried that anyone reading it would assume she'd encouraged him. She convinced Gerald that they no longer needed Paul in the garden; she pretended not to see Paul if she passed him in the supermarket, though she still waved at Jan Biga if they were both out on the street. Glancing into their windows, she saw the blue TV, the yellow wallpaper, the paintings crooked on the wall after Lucinda died. The maple tree dressed and undressed, blazing up and down again, while Paul—quiet behind the curtains—grew older, stronger, better-looking, began spending time with girls his own age, acted civil behind his father's lawnmower on Sundays, as if there had never been a letter, as if she had imagined it. Then he moved away to marry, and she was pleased for him, and pleased to have him gone. By the time he moved back—the marriage over, presumably—he was a complete stranger. She'd never hired his taxi; but then, she'd never needed to.

As for the letter, she had torn it immediately into hundreds of pieces, placed those pieces in an envelope, taped the envelope shut, and concealed it in a box of cereal, which went into the bin and was collected early the following Tuesday morning. She lain in bed listening to the garbage truck trundle up and down the street, Gerald snoring, Terry carrying out his bin in a last-minute panic, and all the birds in Paul's aviary greeting the pretty dawn.

Kate, on the couch, her hand still pointing to the house across the road, waited with a look of bright expectation on her face, as if she had offered an extra serving of cake and was watching to see if Eva would be greedy enough to accept it. Imagine her glee if Eva were to say, "There was one strange thing. Paul wrote me a letter." Imagine her looking at her second-grade daughter and remembering Eva saying, "I had my children" and thinking, then, of the letter.

"I know it's dull of me," Eva said. "But, really, they were a very quiet family."

Outside, the people watching the demolition began to applaud—not the way they might at the end of a football match but as they did when one of the Sydney orchestras visited on a regional tour and the townspeople felt obliged to attend the concert. There was liberation in the applause, but also deflation—as if the spectators had expected rapture and, once again, been disappointed.

"That must be the last wall down," Kate said.

It felt to Eva as if the whole life of the Lainey house would now be on display to the world; as if everyone who had ever lived in it was still there, all at once, going about his or her intimate business, completely unaware that the walls were missing. A sort of doll's house. And in the room that everyone knew had been Paul's, people would see him—what? Making his plans? Dreaming his violent dreams? And they would see Josie and Eva in Josie's little bed, loving each other, very gentle, very pure; they would see Mrs. Lainey opening the door (if there were still doors in the Lainey house) and crying out, the two girls sitting up in bed; and, oh, would they watch as the girls pulled on their summer dresses, as Mrs. Lainey took Josie's hand and led her into the front room, as Mr. Lainey said, "All right, Evelyn, you'd better go on home now"?

"Would you like to go outside and see?" Kate asked.

"Oh, no," Eva said.

"Are you sure?" Kate stood and went to the window.

Eva looked again at the photo on the back of the book. Kate's hand was positioned under her chin in a way that made it look as if her head had been impaled on a fleshy spike. That was unkind; then again, Kate had written page after page describing each murder, and the positions of all the bodies when they were found. Eva hadn't read any of those pages, but she knew, from the talk around town, that they were there.

"Reduced to rubble," Kate said. "How does it feel to know it's down?"

Eva regarded the actual Kate, who had propped one knee on the arm of the couch in order to get closer to the window. Her hair was pulled back into a girlish ponytail and, from behind, her creased navy jacket looked like a school blazer. "Would you be pleased? If you were me?" Eva asked, in the voice she had refined over years of teaching: affectionately stern, lightly curious, and prepared at all times for disappointment.

"God, yes," Kate said. Then she turned to look at Eva and gave a short, unexpected laugh. "Of course I would."

Now a new house would be built: larger, uglier, and filled with the inexplicable lives of other people.

"You won't have to look at it every day," Kate said.

Josie lying in the heat under the maple tree, balancing an apple on her forehead, saying, "Never getting married, never never." Every freckle like a small, warm sun.

"Anyone would be relieved," Kate said. She laughed a second time and said, "But I can't quote myself. Let me ask you again, how do *you* feel about the Biga house coming down?"

"The Lainey house," Eva said.

"The Lainey house."

"I feel," Eva said, "completely indifferent."

The front door opened and closed. Gerald and Terry came staggering in, each carrying a milk crate full of bricks that were the russet color of the Lainey house.

"I'm going to build you an outdoor bread oven," Gerald said.

Kate turned off her Dictaphone.

Terry grinned above his crate, as if he could already feel the oven's heat. Eva looked at him and thought she wouldn't save him, Terry Jarrett—not even if his house were on fire.

FOUR POEMS

WILLIAM ARCHILA

Beyond Bruegel's Shore

Somewhere in Nicaragua or Guatemala
it doesn't matter, his wings ache
rom so much wax, so much discord
in his father's voice, how once
he fled the wards of the state
through air & sky; so simple
& so exact he fell from the clouds
yet no one cared; not the hospitals
not the impoverished nor the imprisoned.
For years, the diagrams of his nerves
branched in confinement. And yet
he has begun a new life
one of labor, of wife & child
his house asleep by the shore, a few
cattle battering the fattening ground.
But something has begun to crack
that dizzy spell of mist, that depth
sweeping over him, blaring in the dark
that thick, rough side of the sea.
This time he set up his gear
because he had to, with no choice
but to curse the coming waters.
This time he swooped so low
he could finger the waves, dropped so low
the foam soaked his hull of feathers.
It's just as well, he banished
it all to the barn. The plowing goes on
but today in Central America it does matter
another boy fell from the sky, chicken fluff & all
body tangled, indeed body tangled.
And there was no one around.

This field of weeds & wildflowers

If I were a painter, I'd start with blue   the color field
as in Sonny Rollins' Colossus. As in Ruben Dario's Azul.
Shelve it. If this were a landscape   thick over thin

intended   or less ornate than a volcano, I'd say
blue like the midday sky or the midday heart

all the birds in Central America madcap. If I had a choice
this oil.   This water.   This lank tool I fool

in my fingers, I'd say the theatrical   blue flame
in a gas stove. Like the black & blue

on my torso, the enormity of it, the batons & asphalt
in blue uniforms.   This Vick's VapoRub jar   clad

on my grandmother's bedside   this asteroid snug fit
in a gravesite   darker than soot, darker

than the coiled look of feathered things.   Her morning walk
her morning song   down the hallway   the mud, the match

when she joined the landscape of birds.   This field
of weeds & wildflowers   let me brush

my hand over the canvas   like in a mirror   how faithful
the camphor.   Her eucalyptus. Her mint

I sniff & smear   on my nostrils. All the blood tint
this cold   blue pigment   all the ink   blue

as a painter   who wipes stained fingers   on her apron.

Spanish Lesson with a Handful of Dirt

Todos vuelven a la tierra en que nacieron —Ruben Blades

You can always claim your roots
in a country once you bury the dead
or is it your dead will claim you always
once you bury your country. I think
bury the dead & your country roots
will bury you is a variation nailed
& final. If Ruben can return in one song
perhaps I can return in a sentence
maybe the word in Spanish for return
or just *recordar* from the Latin *re-cordis*.
No matter, after my father disappeared
wearing a light shirt & dark colored pants
I started listening to his records, sounds
between the conga & the piano player.
Did you know Ruben reminded everyone
during the Cold War it was too hot
in Central America? I do not understand
this lust of how to kill a man. They broke
my father by the alleyway, something
ghastly, even Dante trembled in his pity.
Did the Bible say don't talk to the dead.
They are many & they want out. I think
my father said it best when he told me
you don't have to teach the dead to talk.
They know what to say. They say spring.
They say summer leaves & a handful of dirt.
They might disappear, go back to wherever
they came from, just when you realize
you're accustomed to their sounds.

Our Mouths, Laurels & Lilies

in the slump of the street   they shot him
necklace down   cologne & golden watch

down with his cargo bike   the bullet's nose
broke the sun's sweat   the shot's echo

hit the back of our heads   like ants
we all scattered to the ground   to the kitchen

floor   down the gutter   our teeth nailed
our teeth black   against the graveyard

under the bed   hide under the bed
my cousin said   they shot him   & now

he has rocks in his mouth   laurels & lilies
round his face   the wind's moisture

against his tiny window   a fragment
of darkness   down he went   quietly down

the thud's echo   hit the back of our heads
all our pores on the casket   we touched

the periphery of the earth   we lit matches
spread like mist   neolithic over the streets

FIVE POEMS

MATHEW ZAPRUDER

FOR YOUNG POETS

People talk about flowers
all the time just like
they talk about nuns
and pianos but hardly
anyone can explain exactly
what they are for
how exactly they work
do they choose to go
into the cloister
and become a certain
hue the sun can pass
through attracting notes
that come from a wire
struck by a wooden hammer
or did they hear
a voice once or for many
years that said if you
focus all your love
on this single blade
that doesn't
feel anything something
will fly by and touch
your keys with powder
on its wings and make
music only you were
destined to hear
in the meadow when
you hear it stay there
and wait your calyx
will open it's true
when it does no

matter what they say
there will still be time
for just a little while
keep that music
for yourself

DIRTY TESLA

on the train I ride
through a cloud
the conductor says
as if to me
there are many opportunities
to smoke in Sacramento
and then in Reno,
which seemed truer
than anything,
you pass so quickly
said a pine
and now we are passing
through a piece of California
where people ate each other,
I do not resist
the urge to say aloud
to the lake
down there
that it sounds
like the party
got out of hand,
far below
a blue eye
regards me not,
speaking of history
Dirty Tesla
was the name
of someone's band
in high school,
just like a poem
to a few people
it meant everything
then suddenly ended,
don't tell anyone
who is not here

how some things
do that and others
just get more
obvious in their
malevolence
while we sit here
thinking about
doing everything
with no results,
why are we doing
whatever this is
here in this column
of darkness,
no one knows
except future
scholars of odes
to the final days
in which I never
tire of falling asleep
is what I say
I am telling myself
from the past,
speaking of history
my son attends
a school named
for the first
Californian to die
in what they called
the Great War,
they didn't know
it was only the first,
as soon it started
it already
would continue,
his name was Egbert
followed by a mysterious W,

his poor mother
stood up so straight
in the photograph
of the funeral,
I don't know if he ever
put on one of those
striped suits and went
to look at the sea
before he crossed it
in a boat
full of fellow soldiers,
I just know he died
in a field near
a town called Bony,
all this I relate
to my love as we walk
by the school
the building so utterly
quiet in pre
election summer,
the sign shining
Beach Elementary
back at no one,
it's so sad she said
when everyone thinks
you're a place
but you're a person,
the kaleidoscope
turned again,
we were going
as slowly as we could
toward the tea shop
owned by a friend
named Grace
where all too soon
we would drink

tea made from
what tasted
like the final
chrysanthemums
grown in Fresno

LA PLAGUE

The funniest thing that happened
in high school French was not me bringing
an elaborate bûche de Noël i.e. a Christmas cake
shaped like a log and covered
in chocolate whipped cream my parents
stayed up all night making
for my classmates who stared at what was
suddenly all too unmistakably
a massive poo I had to cut up
and hand to them one by one their faces
distorted in various attempts not to weep
nor when Lars inexplicably fell
out of his chair and shouted
in perfectly accented Spanish mierda!
nor the two weeks the substitute
sat buried in a romance novel
while I along with he who was forced
to be known as Pierre for his name
without gallic equivalent was Brendan
systematically threw
every Victor Hugo one by one
out of the back window onto the cars
parked in the teachers' lot and each time
they made the exact same most
objectively correlated immensely
satisfying thud yes those
astounding moments still
after 35 years shine but the best
was when Eric was asked naturellement
in French by the terrifying Mme. Kitzes
what he thought of the book
by Camus we were supposed to have read
all weekend instead of imagining
somewhere there was some party we almost
got invited to instead of with grim

determination masturbating to the soft
tones of Aztec Camera and he called it
La Plague instead of La Peste
which made it absolutely clear
that if he had considered reading
anything at all it was that little red book
in English we had somehow all
managed to procure and Mme. Kitzes
looked at him with absolute middle-aged
homicidal grief I have many times
felt myself now that I am whatthe leaders of this webinar I currently
have the responsitunity to watch
call an educator and none of us could stop
laughing at ourselves which in those
holy wasted days was everything.

THUS

I don't know why
I keep thinking
of my first car,
so dark and green
the perfect color
for disappearing
at night into the deep
park with its roads
that led to friends,
the mystery
of their kindness,
without a thought
I let them all go,
it was so old
but carried me
across the quadrate
capital where
I was born,
I drove through
shadows giant white
buildings cast,
sometimes spring
blossoms from famous
trees the mayor
of Tokyo gave us long
before the war
on my windshield
fell, one winter
when I was young
the radio told me
a plane crashed
into the bridge
then the DJ made
a terrible joke
and I laughed,

was that when
I began to snow,
a thousand years
of ice covered
my path, before
I ever found it
I lost even my
thought of home,
if from the provinces
I should return
I will drive
to the bridge,
stop and get out
wearing the black
luxurious coat
with a torn
lining my father
gave away,
touch the railing,
look down in the dark
the water contains
and wonder
where did
the bodies go,
will they pull them
out or wait
until spring,
what calculations,
are you still there
under the dark,
should I destroy
this mountain
of snow on my hand,
the buildings with
their vacancies
beckon but I must

stay here just a few
centuries longer,
who first told me
about that meadow
no one has found
without falling
asleep to forget
all the most
beloved ones,
terrible meadow
where I went
to be safe
from my only
ones who will
keep me safe,
how much longer
must I stay here
in this meadow
the blue bees visit,
to them all
flowers are strange,
they love no one
thus and thus
they do no harm.

ELEGY FOR A COSMONAUT

for Dean Young

The year you were born silver birches
tapped on the window
and the curve of a nail clipper
caught some light from a distant star
where gentle beings look down
and shake their heads
the year you learned to speak
you wrote your first poem
and hard-working ghosts
used old technology
to create a blue unity
in no way essential to a life of metaphor
the year you got your new heart
the huge god in the mural agreed
it is sad to be only half machine
and live in a future
that belonged to someone else
the year you disappeared
in the marriage of street signs
and a convoy asleep in rain
I finally understood
why you said they say
the little wren is the one
who sings the most notes
but tell that to the bench
carved with all those names
tell that to the sandwich
of glittering water
the year you died I almost resisted
a yellow flower successfully
the year you died it was Tuesday
I touched the spines of your books
their once pale colors now bright
and I heard at last
that distant apiary filling
with the echo of replacement

ARE YOU HAPPY?

A STORY

LORI OSTLUND

Twenty-four years after the crash, Phil would return to Albuquerque to see his mother and she would ask whether he was happy. She was in the final stages of stomach cancer by then, living—or, more accurately, dying—in his brother's house, and Phil sat there, not sure how to answer her question because they'd never talked about such things. Happiness. She'd always scoffed at people who did, maintaining that happiness was a uniquely American preoccupation, speaking as if she were not American. Even then, at the end of her life, Phil believed she would hold an admission of happiness against him.

He had awakened that morning at home in San Francisco, Kelvin and their whole menagerie huddled around him, his legs stiff from being curled up to accommodate the cats, who stretched across the middle of the bed, rejecting parallelism because they preferred to sleep perpendicular. "Daddy's going away today," Kelvin loud-whispered, phrasing that always struck Phil as vaguely but disturbingly sexual, the *Daddy*-part he supposed. The dogs leaped up and began bouncing between them. It was "away" that got them going—Kelvin had trained them to associate the word with car rides—but Phil liked to pretend that it was his imminent departure to which they were responding.

"Let's all eat breakfast together on the raft," Kelvin said. *The raft* was what he called their bed. It was king-size. "We're a growing family," he'd said when they bought it. They were up to seven now: the two of them, three cats, two dogs. Each night at bedtime, Kelvin called out, "Everyone on the raft," and all seven of them climbed on. There, surrounded by a chorus of snorting and snoring and purring, Kelvin always fell asleep quickly, as if the raft were meandering down a peaceful river, while Phil lay wide awake most nights, gripping the mattress as the current quickened, pulling him toward the rapids.

That morning, the morning that Phil would get on the plane to visit his dying mother, Kelvin got up and brought them all breakfast, arranging the bowls of kibble strategically across the comforter, isolating Ollie, their fat boy, who was fond of sniffing the others' buttocks to distract them and then stealing their food. "Let's have sex," declared Kelvin when they were done eating because he never felt shy about making his desire known, and he got out of bed again, stacked all seven bowls on the dresser, and herded the animals out of the room. Ollie had to be picked up and dropped just as the door was being shut behind him because even though he was portly, he was quick. "You do know they're sitting out there listening," Kelvin said as he returned to the bed. Banning them was not his idea. "Besides, sex is perfectly natural."

"Sex is natural," Phil agreed, though he did not believe this for a minute. There was nothing natural about the way people's faces contorted in the throes of an orgasm or how they seemed as pleasant and agreeable as door-to-door salesmen beforehand, then cold and occasionally cruel after. Kelvin was the first man he'd met who wanted the same things before and after, in bed and out: intimacy and pleasure and reciprocity.

He reached for Kelvin. "But you want me to enjoy myself, right? And I can assure you that I stop enjoying myself the minute Alfie starts howling along."

Kelvin leaped on top of Phil. "Woof," he said. He burrowed his face in Phil's crotch, and Phil laughed.

The call from work came just as they finished, an emergency that Phil could have asked one of the other vets to attend to, but the family had requested him. Kelvin had taken the day off work—he had a boring but flexible office job—to drive him to the airport, so they rose and dressed and went first to the clinic, where Kelvin waited in the car with Alfie and Madeline while Phil handled the emergency, and from there to the airport. As they stood at the curb saying good-bye, Kelvin began to cry. He looked right at Phil as he sobbed, even stroking his cheek, while the curbside baggage checker stood several feet away, staring and scowling. Phil pretended to focus on his husband, though all he could think about was the baggage checker.

The dogs put their snouts out the half-open car window and began whimpering. "You see?" Kelvin said, his face still wet. "The whole family's miserable."

This—the way Kelvin spoke, without sarcasm or subtext—could have turned Phil off all those years ago when they first met, but instead it had seemed exotic, inviting. When Phil joked with him on one of their first dates, "My god, you're as earnest as a lesbian," Kelvin laughed because it could be both funny and true. Phil discovered that he liked making Kelvin laugh. As a boy, he'd never made people laugh, except at him. This was particularly true of his family, who laughed at him often and considered him overly sensitive for minding.

He met Kelvin at an auction, a fundraiser for an animal shelter at which he'd volunteered when he first moved to Davis, after he'd fled New Mexico and his family and the life he was expected to live there. At the time of the auction, he was in veterinary school, and the listing in the auction program read: *Date with sexy veterinarian student!* A group of women with whom he volunteered had come up with the idea, and though the whole thing embarrassed him greatly, he'd gone along with it, which meant that halfway through the evening he found himself up on the stage being told to strike a sexy vet pose. Mainly, the bidders were women his mother's age—*bidding biddies*, he thought, ungenerously. It did not surprise him that bidding biddies were his audience. What did surprise him was the lone man, Bidder 13, who kept lifting his paddle until most of the bidding biddies had dropped away and it became a duel between him and a woman in her sixties wearing cat ears and whiskers. Finally, the man threw down his paddle in defeat. This was Kelvin.

After the auction was over and Phil was standing to the side of the buffet table with Carol, the shelter receptionist, Kelvin approached him, pausing—out of nervousness or hunger—to select a shrimp-and-cucumber canapé. He stood in front of Phil, his face a deep red, which Phil misread as shyness until Carol said, "I think he's choking." She'd spent the last five minutes referring to Phil as the *975-Dollar Man*, which is what the cat woman had paid for the date, but her voice turned serious then, the way it got when someone brought in a sick animal they'd found on the street.

"Are you choking?" Phil asked, and Kelvin nodded.

Phil pounded him on the back, and when this did not work, he put his arms around Kelvin from behind, placed a fist above Kelvin's navel, and administered the Heimlich Maneuver, jerking up so hard that

Kelvin's feet came off the ground. He did this twice more, and Carol said, "I think you got it."

Kelvin nodded in agreement and spit the shrimp back into his hand. "You're amazing," he said to Phil when he could finally talk, and Phil buttoned his suit coat to hide the fact that he was aroused, turned on by this whole unlikely version of himself.

—

His brother Tom had someone waiting for him at the airport in Albuquerque, an employee from the family business that Phil had fled all those years ago. The man was in his thirties, nervous and deferential, no doubt assuming that Phil was like his brother. He drove Phil to Tom's house, which was predictably large and nondescript. Tom was there waiting for him—already bundled into his coat—and after the brothers shook hands, Tom left, like they were factory co-workers passing between shifts.

Phil had never been to his brother's house. He went into the living room, where he stood considering the décor, which made sense neither aesthetically nor in terms of what he knew of his brother, who had always valued practicality. There were numerous ceramic reproductions of books, all crudely cast, and above the fake fireplace, framed behind glass, an arrangement of potholders. Potholders! He supposed that Sandra, Tom's wife, whom he had met just twice, might be responsible for the décor. He went over to the rocking chair beside the fireplace, but as soon as he sat down, Sandra appeared, and he stood back up. She, too, shook his hand, then explained with some urgency that the chair in which he'd been sitting was "just for show." He did not know what this meant, but remained standing.

After that, neither of them spoke, and when the hospice nurse arrived for her daily visit, Sandra put on her coat and left, so it was the hospice nurse who led him down the hallway to the guestroom, in the middle of which stood a hospital bed. There, tucked into the bed, was his mother. She opened her eyes and said, "Oh, it's you," as though she'd seen him just minutes earlier, but he made a point to go over to her and kiss her forehead.

The nurse showed him everything—a list of instructions, broken down by the hour; the packets of nutritional shakes that his mother did not want to drink but needed to; a drawer filled with oral syringes of pain medicine—all while writing on charts and attending to his mother, who alternated between ordering the nurse around and ignoring her. The nurse did not hurry or become impatient, and when she was done with her visit, Phil walked her to the door and thanked her in an apologetic voice.

"She's not so bad," the nurse said. "At least she knows what she wants."

Phil laughed in agreement.

"And she's much calmer, now that you're here. She's been anxious for you to arrive." This, he knew, was one of those things that medical people say, a one-size-fits-all approach that treated the world as a place where families were happiest together.

Some of his friends had told him that the hardest thing about a parent's death was that the argument suddenly ended, but in his case the argument had never really begun. He had withdrawn from the debate, left without telling his family that he was going, eventually contacting them to say that he had settled in California. When he met Kelvin, he let the answering machine announce his relationship—*You have reached the home of Phil and Kelvin*—and his family never asked for details. When Kelvin wanted to accompany him on his infrequent visits back home, he declined, saying, "I'm saving you from them," but the truth was that he was saving himself. As long as Kelvin was not there—sitting at their table asking questions about what Phil had been like as a boy and expecting to sleep in Phil's childhood bed with him at night—they did not have to discuss any of it.

At the airport that morning, the last thing Kelvin said was "Call if you need me to come." He tried to imagine Kelvin here, in his brother's house, wondered how his mother would feel, dying with a stranger beside her. But wasn't he a stranger also?

He waved as the hospice nurse drove off, then went back into the guestroom. His mother's eyes were shut, and he sat down in a chair, relieved. It was then, without opening her eyes, that his mother asked whether he was happy. When he didn't answer, she said, "I suppose it was a good thing you ran away like that, even if you just turned your back on everything—your father, the business." She spoke as if they were discussing recent events, not events that had occurred years ago.

"I told your father all along you weren't cut out for it—the business. You never liked the direct approach to anything."

Her eyes were still closed, and she sighed deeply.

"Actually, I don't think your father was even disappointed," she went on, either trying to goad him or just talking, which often sounded like the same thing. Kelvin, who was unapologetically influenced by pop psychology texts, said that falling into established family patterns of communication was a self-fulfilling prophecy, that it was within Phil's control to respond differently, a position with which Phil—in theory and from a distance—agreed. In practice, at this particular moment, he said nothing. "The truth is he was probably relieved that you left."

"You know what?" Phil said suddenly. "I *am* happy. Kelvin and I have a wonderful life together. Is that direct enough for you?"

His mother opened her eyes but did not look at him. "You let that crash get the better of you," she said.

—

After the shuttle dropped them at the hotel the day of the crash, the three of them—Phil, his mother, and his aunt—went upstairs to the rooms they'd been assigned by the airline and into the smaller of the two, which Phil assumed was his because it had just one bed. None of them had luggage—it was gone with the plane—and Phil felt even more lost without a bag to unpack, toiletries to arrange. He waited, but his mother and aunt did not go into the adjoining room. They just stood there. Finally, his mother drew the curtains closed and climbed into the king-size bed that was supposed to be his, and he and his aunt followed. Except for their shoes, they got in fully dressed, his mother in the middle, mirroring their seating on the plane. It was ironic that they had been sitting that way, for they all three accepted that it was his aunt's job to buffer Phil and his mother from each other, but his aunt needed to be at the window, looking out. She said it was how she kept the plane afloat. Of course, this was ironic also.

The overhead light was on, but no one got up to shut it off. Nobody spoke. What was there to say? None of them wanted to relive the moments just before the crash, or the chaos after. And before that? Before that, they had been on vacation, drinking and laughing under the bright

Caribbean sun. Now, they were huddled beneath the blankets, their teeth chattering hard in their mouths. At some point, Phil rose and went into the adjoining room, where he stripped the comforters from both beds, brought them back, and covered his mother and aunt. For the first time in his life, he felt like an adult.

They stayed in bed together for thirty-six hours. Phil did not sleep. Each time he closed his eyes, he felt the plane beneath him, speeding down the runway, the backward tilt as its nose poked upward, the plane hesitating, then falling back, hard. Around him, people had screamed; he had screamed with them.

The morning of the second day, the telephone rang and Phil got out of bed and answered it. It was the airline, checking on them.

"Have you arranged a flight for us?" he asked the woman on the other end.

Directly after the crash, the survivors had been brought to a room at the airport set up with coffee and telephones. Phil and his mother had called his father back home, explaining that there had been an accident. Phil's father was at his office, and even though he was on the phone with his wife and son who were calling because they had almost died, he held the receiver between his ear and shoulder and waved to his secretary to bring him some paperwork that needed signing—or so Phil imagined, given his father's distracted response. For his father, even tragedy could be multitasked.

Phil waited for the airline woman to answer his question, to say that she had booked a flight for the three of them, even though he could not imagine getting back on a plane so soon, maybe ever. Instead, she hiccupped loudly. She did not apologize, but he supposed the ensuing silence had to do with her feeling embarrassed, hiccupping like that into the ear of a crash victim.

"We can't arrange flights quite yet," said the airline representative at last. "We're still identifying bodies." She paused. "That's actually why I'm calling—we need someone from your party to come to the morgue."

"Party?" he said loudly, finding the word strange, almost offensive, in a conversation about morgues and bodies. He was sitting on the edge of the bed, still wearing the clothes he'd had on for the flight—jeans with a button-down shirt and linen jacket, in deference to his mother, who insisted that flying was something you dressed up for. She and his aunt wore skirts, which rode up around their thighs when they slid to safety; now, beneath the layers of blankets, he imagined their skirts had done the same. "I'll come," he said to the airline woman.

"Who was it, Philip?" his mother asked.

"The airline," he said. "I need to, you know, identify their bodies."

When he returned two hours later, his mother and aunt were out of bed, showered, and dressed in clothes that the airline had delivered. Phil had never seen his mother in a T-shirt. Neither woman asked about the morgue, which was fine with him. He did not want to discuss any of it, to hear himself using words like *fungi* to describe how Mr. Milford's left ear had looked, melted to the side of his head.

"Philip," said his mother, "will you take us out for a late lunch, please?"

She had never spoken to him like this, requesting rather than demanding his services. Though his homosexuality was not discussed between them, she treated him like her homosexual son nonetheless, expecting him to escort her to dinner and concerts, on shopping excursions and to the hair salon. Art, the man with whom he was having sex back home in Albuquerque, had told him he needed to learn how to stand up for himself, stop being such a sissy. Art was ashamed of him. Whenever they went out in public, which was rarely, Art walked several feet ahead of him, pretending they were not together.

Art did not walk this way with his wife. Phil had seen them once, strolling along Central with their two children. In bed later that week, when Phil asked Art what his children's names were, Art smashed Phil's head into the headboard. "You think I want their names coming out of your filthy faggot mouth?" Art said.

Phil had wanted to say something clever about what Art wanted from his filthy faggot mouth. "No," he said instead, soothingly. "Of course not."

"Lunch, yes," Phil answered his mother. "Let me just get out of these clothes." He picked up the bag that the airline had left for him and took it into the bathroom. Inside were T-shirts, extra-large though he was a medium at best, imprinted with the airline's logo. He put one on. He looked like a walking advertisement for an airline that had nearly killed him.

The bed was made, neatly, and his mother and aunt sat on it, waiting. "I haven't gone out without a purse since I was a girl," his mother was saying to his aunt. They had obeyed orders to leave everything behind when they evacuated, though in the survivors' room afterward, some women sat clutching their purses, symbols of their betrayal. His mother had surprised him, not because she'd left hers—she was a stickler for rules—but because she refrained from commenting on those who had not.

They had only what was in Phil's pockets—some leftover vacation currency and his credit card—but they avoided the hotel restaurant, where the airline was running a tab, and instead took a taxi to a nearby restaurant. They needed to be away from the other survivors, though they did not say this aloud.

As they finished their first course, two businessmen sat down at the table next to them and began to smoke. "How's your soup?" Phil asked his mother to distract her from the smoking.

"Mine is very good," said his aunt, doing the same.

"Excuse me," his mother called to the men. "Please put those out. We're trying to eat." She waved her hand at the cigarettes, and the men laughed.

"Americans, no?" said the younger man.

"Yes," said Phil.

"Americans are always the pure ones in the room," said the older man, sweeping his arm to indicate the other tables, which were occupied by people smoking and drinking and laughing. "But sometimes you just need to live a little instead of thinking every cigarette is going to kill you." He raised his wineglass at them encouragingly.

His mother stood and walked past the men as though she were leaving, but before Phil and his aunt could rise to follow her, she turned back around and went right up to the men's table. "You see me here in front of you?" she said. "I am living."

—

The Milfords were dead, dead because they smoked. That was the melodramatic way to think of it but also the truth. They had all boarded the plane together, but when Phil, his mother, and aunt reached the fifth row, they waved good-bye to the Milfords, and the Milfords waved cheerfully back as they continued toward the smoking section at the rear of the plane, the section that would be crushed when the plane dropped back on its tail. As the Milfords moved down the aisle, Phil turned and saw Mr. Milford press his hand lightly to his wife's back. The night before, as the five of them sat in the resort lounge after their final dinner together, Mr. Milford had reached under the table and pressed that same hand to Phil's thigh. Phil's first thought was that Mr. Milford had somehow mixed up right and left, believed that he was caressing his wife's thigh as he stared straight ahead, listening to Phil's mother explain what was wrong with vegetarians, which was that they didn't eat meat. In response, Mr. Milford laughed, but Phil knew his mother was not being clever. She was rarely intentionally funny and never with topics that angered her, like vegetarians.

"I don't trust anyone who doesn't eat meat," said Mr. Milford, his hand climbing higher on Phil's thigh. Belatedly, Phil realized that the comment was intended for him. In those days, Phil was often surprised by people, perplexed by the things they said and did. But had he truly been surprised by Mr. Milford's hand that night? Just hours earlier at the pool, Mr. Milford had chatted with him the way an uncle might, even as he regarded the pouch in Phil's swimming trunks with a steady, almost amused gaze. Phil was used to men being startled by his size, not just the few, generally straight men with whom he'd had furtive sex but all the men he'd ever been obligated to shower beside, in high school and then college. They watched him mince toward the showers, penis swinging like an elephant's trunk, startled but also, he thought, angered at the injustice.

He did not remove Mr. Milford's hand. He didn't know why exactly, except that it was already there, *situated*. Then, Mr. Milford's wife jumped up. "ABBA!" she screamed. "Let's dance, Rob."

Mr. Milford's hand stopped its cajoling and joined his other hand, which was raised in mock protest, but Mrs. Milford—Kate, she'd insisted Phil call her—pulled her husband from his chair anyway. The lounge was dim, but Mr. Milford's crotch, when he stood, was at eye level, so Phil could see the effect the encounter had had on him. Phil's own crotch had registered nothing, which both pleased and baffled him. He supposed it was that his mother was sitting right there across from him, sipping cognac and saying, "I've never cared for legumes."

When Mr. Milford came to his room later that night to finish the furtive fumbling he'd started under the table, Phil invited him in. The sex was fast and not quite as rough as Phil had come to expect from straight men, which was how he regarded Mr. Milford because he had a wife. Afterward, they lay together on the bed and talked. It felt strange and intimate and exhilarating. Mr. Milford lit two cigarettes and passed him one. He showed Phil how to draw the smoke in, hold it, and blow it back out, and Phil followed his instructions, all the while recalling the straightforward dictums from his childhood about the perils of smoking. He'd always trusted straightforward dictums.

Eventually, they had sex again, more slowly this time. When they were finished, Mr. Milford turned toward him, propping his head on his arm. He studied Phil: his body and then his face. "You're such a lovely boy," he said.

"Thank you," Phil said, in a polite voice that made Mr. Milford laugh, and Phil felt compelled to add, "Actually, I'm twenty-two. I just finished college."

Of course, Mr. Milford knew this already. At dinner the first night, when the two families were seated together, his mother had told the Milfords all sorts of things, including how she had presented Phil with the trip as a surprise graduation present, not mentioning that she had done so even though she knew that he hated resorts, hated lying on the beach and sharing the rarified air of the resort grounds with people who thought themselves experts on a host of third-world countries because they had frequented their resorts. The two families had made plans to meet again the next day, the week taking shape around their new friendship, around some daily configuration of the five of them eating and shopping and going on excursions. When they discovered that they were even booked on the same flight out—a discount shuttle that flew between the resort island and Puerto Rico—they regarded it less as a coincidence than one last outing that they had planned together.

There in bed, he and Mr. Milford did not discuss their departure the next morning or anything having to do with the five of them. "What do you plan to do next?" Mr. Milford asked. "Do you have a job lined up?"

"I'm going to work at my father's business," Phil said. He tried to sound nonchalant.

"Business?" said Mr. Milford. "I don't see you in business." He added, "I don't mean that in a bad way."

"I told you I studied business in college," Phil said. "It's been the plan for both of us, me and my brother, since we were boys."

"I see," said Mr. Milford. He stroked Phil's arm, and Phil wondered where Mrs. Milford—Kate—thought her husband was. "But what would *you* choose? What is it that you want to do?"

"I'm a pragmatist," said Phil. This was not true. He was a romantic, and he did not think one could be both. "Anyway, I'm already enough of a disappointment because of, you know." He gestured at the two of them side by side on the bed, naked. This was the image he would recall as he stood in the makeshift morgue two and a half days later.

What he wanted to be was a veterinarian. He'd dreamed about it since he was six, when Hans came to live with them. Hans was nothing like the dog that Phil had picked out from the lineup of breeds in the encyclopedia—a dachshund. "We're not getting a damn wiener dog," his father had said, and the next day he came home with Hans, but the thing about Hans was that even though he was a big dog—"a man's dog," his father liked to say—Hans loved *him*. He didn't care that Phil had no friends or that he was a boy who thought about other boys. When Phil lay in bed crying, Hans came, and when Phil wrapped his arms around Hans, Hans curled against him and stayed that way, steady and warm, through the night.

He did not tell Mr. Milford any of this that night, but five days later, when he and his mother and aunt finally arrived back in Albuquerque, he got off the plane and went directly to his apartment, packed his car, and drove west to California, then north to Davis, where he found a job working at an animal clinic and volunteered at the shelter. Two years later, he started veterinary school, and then he met Kelvin. He tried not to think about the fact that his own happiness had come about because Mr. Milford died.

—

The first time Phil went out to dinner with Kelvin's parents, they had on matching T-shirts with the words *We Love Our Gay Son*. Phil asked whether this meant that they did not love Kelvin's brother, who was straight, and they laughed as though he were joking. He supposed he was. The next time, they had new shirts: *We Love Our Gay Son and His Gay Boyfriend.* They sat in the restaurant wearing their public displays of support and eating the calamari appetizer. "Phil," they asked, "how does your family respond to your homosexuality?"

"By not talking about it," he replied, keeping his tone light, but Kelvin's parents drew closer. "These things can't just be brushed under the rug," his mother said. She set down a forkful of tentacles and lifted the corner of her placemat, pretending to sweep breadcrumbs under it with her other hand.

"Would it help if we spoke to them?" Kelvin's father said. "We're happy to give them a call."

"I couldn't ask you do that," Phil said. "I don't even like talking to them." He laughed, but it ended in a high-pitched squeak that threatened to devolve into tears. His father had always responded to his tears by saying, "I'll give you something to cry about" and then proceeding to do so. Once, when he was twelve, his father had yanked down his pants and spanked him right there in the plaza in Old Town as tourists walked by, his buttocks heating up beneath his father's blows and the steady New Mexico sun. The memory was as vivid as the expressions of concern on the faces of Kelvin's parents as they stared at him. He'd looked away, down at their T-shirts. *I love your gay son also*, he thought. He thought about how he would never declare this on a T-shirt. He was crying, and he stood up from the table, pushed back his chair, and left.

Not even a year later, he and Kelvin had moved to San Francisco because he understood by then that he was not cut out to be part of a happy family either. Each month, Kelvin's parents drove into the city to stay with them, and Phil wondered whether they knew that they were the reason for the move. He didn't think so because during these visits, when Kelvin called out, "Everyone on the raft," Kelvin's mother came into their room and lay at the foot of the bed, talking to them as she stroked Ollie's fat stomach, and then she would get up and kiss them both goodnight.

—

In her hospital bed, his mother lay turned away from him. He thought she might be crying. He had not seen her cry in the twenty-four years since the crash, not even when his father had died a year earlier. That night, the night his father died, he and Kelvin sat down to eat dinner and Phil said, "Just so you know, the phone's going to ring any minute, but we're not going to answer it."

"Okay," said Kelvin, not asking because he knew by now how this worked, and sure enough, a few minutes later, Phil said, "I did it. You said I needed to, and I did."

"The invitation?" Kelvin said, and Phil said, "Yes," and just like that, the phone rang. They both laughed because there was something funny about saying a thing would happen just before it did. The dogs began to bark, not at the phone but at the laughing. They did not like to be left out.

"We'll let the machine take it," Phil said. He loved answering machines, the sense of control they gave him. "I know it's them. It would have arrived today. I'll call back tomorrow, but for now I just want to feel happy."

He and Kelvin were getting married, finally, after nineteen years, because for the first time, they could, legally that is. There would be a brief ceremony at City Hall followed by a party, and the only catch was that Kelvin said Phil needed to invite his family. "Force *them* to make the decision," he said. "Don't make it for them."

"Call me," said his mother's voice from the corner of the room in his tiny house where his mother had never been. "I need to tell you something."

She sounded strange, a different kind of strange from the strange that had to do with responding to an invitation to the wedding of your homosexual son, and he called immediately. "What's up?" he said, and she said, "It's your father."

"What about him?" He was expecting her to say that his father had told her to call, had made it her job to explain that they had no intention of attending this "wedding"—"wedding," her tone would make clear, in quotation marks.

"He's dead," she said. "The ambulance is here, so I better go. I just thought you'd want to know."

"Dead?" he said. He'd never imagined his father in those terms. "How?"

"He was sitting at the table, eating dinner and looking through the mail. I went into the kitchen to get him another piece of lasagna, and when I came back he was gone."

She paused. "Oh, there was something from you today. Some sort of invitation." Her voice made clear that this was the end of *that* conversation.

As he and Kelvin lay in bed later that night, Phil said, "Do you think it was, you know, because of the invitation?"

"What?" said Kelvin sleepily, and then, "You mean the heart attack?"

That was exactly what he meant.

"Oh, Philip. No. Heart attacks don't work that way." Kelvin took his hand in the dark. "I can't believe your mother, that she had the presence of mind to bring up the invitation as they were carrying your father's body out of the house."

From her hospital bed just one year later, his mother said, "Whatever happened with that invitation, the one that arrived the day your father died?"

He'd always imagined dying as a tunnel that narrowed around you until everything ceased to exist and it was just you, walking alone, no longer caring what those around you said or thought or ate for lunch or even who the next president was going to be, but maybe he'd been wrong. "You're wondering whether Kelvin and I got married?" he asked.

She was still turned away from him, but she was definitely crying, and he pulled back the covers and got into bed beside his mother.

"Philip?" she said. She sounded alarmed.

"Yes," he said. "I'm here." He made his voice soothing, like he was talking to an injured animal.

After a while, his mother said, "Do you remember those men at the restaurant? The ones who wouldn't stop smoking?" She sounded calmer, and he thought that she had forgotten about wanting to know whether he was married. He *was* married, but he wasn't going to insist on telling her.

"Yes," he said. "I remember."

"They made me so mad." She laughed, and he laughed with her.

"I mainly remember how you went over to their table and yelled at them," he said. "I admired you so much at that moment." He realized this was true.

"Really?" she said. "I was sure I'd embarrassed you."

His brother would be home any minute. He would come into the bedroom, take in the sight of Philip in bed with their dying mother, and say, "What are you doing?," his brother who could not differentiate between practical and beautiful.

Phil shifted onto his side toward his mother. Her eyes were closed, but he could see that she was in pain. It was his job to understand pain. "Are you afraid?" he asked.

She did not answer, and he thought maybe she'd dozed off. "No," she said at last. "What would be the use? I just want it to be over."

"Don't say that," he said, a perfunctory response.

"There's nothing more for me here. I'm just waiting to die, and you know I've never liked waiting." She paused. "I'm glad you're here, Phillip."

Kelvin had told him that people sometimes softened before death, that they understood—maybe only then—what they'd wished for from life.

"I'm glad, too," he said. He was.

Only now did his mother open her eyes. "Listen. I need you to give me all of it," she said, pointing at the drawer where the pain medicine was kept, several weeks' worth, the oral syringes lined up like the hulls of wingless planes. "No one will wonder," she said. "The hospice people left it, after all," and then, when he didn't answer, "Really, Philip. I thought you'd gotten over all of that. Your timidity."

The emergency he'd been called in to deal with on his way to the airport that morning had involved a dog, just four years old, with a tumor that had proven inoperable. Phil had not known the dog or the family well. They were new to the city, but they had asked for him. The dog reared up just once, when Phil pushed the needle into his back leg. The family gathered around, crying unabashedly, Phil crying with them. "He was a lovely boy," he'd said, Mr. Milford's voice still with him after all these years.

"It's not that," he told his mother. "I'm not worried about getting caught." He thought about all the creatures he'd put down, the relief he'd sensed in their bodies at the very end. "It's just—You're my mother," he said finally, though he knew that this was no reason at all.

CONTRIBUTORS

William Archila is the winner of the 2023 Philip Levine Prize for Poetry for his collection *S is For*. He is the author of *The Art of Exile* and *The Gravedigger's Archeology*. He was awarded the 2023 Jack Hazard fellowship. His work has appeared in *AGNI, APR, Copper Nickle, The Georgia Review, Kenyon Review, Prairie Schooner, Poetry, Ploughshares, Poetry Northwest, Pleiades, TriQuarterly* and the anthology *Latino Poetry: The Library of American Anthology*. He has work forthcoming in *New Ohio Review*. He is an associate editor at Tía Chucha Press.

Ingrid Molina Arellano is still working on her bio. She is a student in the Girls Inc of Alameda County workshop.

Chris Feliciano Arnold has written essays and journalism for *The Atlantic, Harper's, The New York Times, Outside, Sports Illustrated, Vice News, The Believer, Folha de S. Paulo* and more. The recipient of a creative writing fellowship from the National Endowment for the Arts, he has published fiction in *Playboy, The Kenyon Review, Ecotone* and other magazines. Along the way, his work has been noted in *The Best American Sports Writing* and *The Best American Short Stories*. He lives in the San Francisco Bay Area where he is Director of the MFA Program in Creative Writing at Saint Mary's College of California. His first book, *The Third Bank of the River: Power and Survival in the Twenty-First Century Amazon*, is a work of narrative nonfiction published by Picador in 2018. Presently, he is at work on a novel and a collection of short stories.

Enaya Buksh, *one of four collaborating poets*, is a 9th grader at LPS, Hayward. She wants to live life to the fullest and is in love with horse riding, swimming, running, and singing. She wants people to read her work and connect with it, in hopes it might promote change.... **Teifa Lam-Triplett** is a 9th grader at LPS, Hayward..... **K. Emmanuelle Mendoza** is currently a 9th-grade student at LPS Hayward. She's an art enthusiast and loves music.... **Sophia Ruiz** is a kind person who likes to help others in the ways she can. She's also a freshman at LPS Hayward who's almost becoming a sophomore. Overall, Sophia shows wonderful traits like respectfulness, humility, and understanding.

Laura Cogan is a freelance editor and nonprofit consultant. She was the Editor and Executive Director of ZYZZYVA, Inc. for over ten years. She serves on the NewLit Board of Directors.

Jennine Capó Crucet (she/her/ella) is a 2025 Recipient of the Joyce Carol Oates Prize. She is a writer and educator. A recipient of a PEN/O. Henry Prize and a former Contributing Opinion Writer for The New York Times, she's the author of four books: the novel *Make Your Home Among Strangers*, which won the International Latino Book Award and has been adopted as an all-campus/community read at over forty U.S. universities; the multiple award-winning story collection *How to Leave Hialeah*; and the essay collection *My Time Among the Whites: Notes from an Unfinished Education*, longlisted for the PEN/Open Book Award. Her most recent book, the critically acclaimed novel *Say Hello to My Little Friend*, was a finalist for the Kirkus Prize for Fiction and the Los Angeles Times Book Prize. Her fiction and nonfiction have been widely anthologized, and her work has appeared on PBS NewsHour, NPR, and other national and international publications. She's worked as a professor of creative writing and has taught workshops at conferences across the country. She's also worked as a screenwriter, a college access counselor to first-generation college students, and as a sketch comedienne (though not all at the same time). Born and raised in Miami, she lives in North Carolina with her family.

Grace Decker is a writer and artist from Northern California. Her work has been previously featured in *Simpsonistas* and *The Gist*. She was once a student in the NewLit Writing Workshop at Northgate High School.

Joseph Di Prisco, Series Editor of *Simpsonistas*, has published six novels, four books of poetry, two memoirs, two works of nonfiction, many poems and reviews and essays in numerous journals, and won a few prizes along the way. He is Founding Chair of the New Literary Project Board of Directors. He received his Ph.D. in English from the University of California, Berkeley, and taught for a long time. His most recent book is *My Last Resume: New & Collected Poems*. (diprisco.com) jdp@newliteraryproject.org

Half Khmer, **Violet Ferreira** uses poetry to express her culture through rhythm, vivid imagery, and nuanced perspectives. Many of the Khmer were killed during the reign of the Khmer Rouge, an extremist communist regime. Under the dictator Pol Pot, Cambodians were denied music, prescription glasses, and oftentimes had to violate ancient Buddhist practices that have been around for millennia. Growing up, Ferreira heard many stories of her ancestors, but never with shame. Her great grandfather, who was killed in a rice field by the Khmer Rouge, was described with a sense of honor for refusing to sacrifice his morals. References to blessing strings (red string worn across the wrist signifying spiritual protection), Apsaras (Mythical heavenly Khmer dancers), and rice farming hold great significance in both Khmer culture and history and are used frequently in her poems. Through poetry, Ferreira imagines a Cambodia untouched by colonialism and extremist politics.

Kalia Griffin is a junior at Albany high school, she has been on the variety softball team since freshman year. She has played softball for about 7 years. Her dream job is to work in a hair salon. She is working on that by cutting and dyeing people's hair in her school and doing her family's hair.

Lyrik Harris is sixteen years old. She grew up as an art and music lover in Richmond, CA.

Lina Ihaddadene is a sixteen-year-old sophomore student at Emery High School, originally from Algeria. She moved to California at the age of thirteen with a dream in her mind. She worked through the differences between the two worlds and found her peace in her mind, thoughts, and actions. Her writings represent her love for horror and curiosity about the supernatural.

Katharine Kho, sixteen, calls Oakland, California home. She carries with her the rich, intertwined roots of Chinese and Laotian heritage.

Hailing from the wet and wild state of Virginia, **Drew Kiser** is a PhD candidate in English at the University of California, Berkeley, exploring the affective history of fossil fuels through Victorian literature and contemporary American film. Before beginning his career in academia,

Drew worked as a baker, farmer, teacher, and political consultant in West Virginia, France, South Africa, and Washington, D.C., respectively.

Ralph J. Long Jr. is the author of *Odes* (forthcoming Main Street Rag Press, 2025) and three chapbooks, *It Doesn't Matter that…* (EXPRESS Digital Chapbooks, 2025); *Polaroids at a Yard Sale* (Main Street Rag Press, 2021) and *A Democracy Divided* (Poetry Box, 2018). His work has appeared in *Anacapa Review, Cloudbank, Common Ground Review, Peregrine, Stoneboat Literary Journal, Sisyphus, South 85 Journal, Ursa Minor, Zingara Poetry Review,* and elsewhere. He was a finalist in the Marsh Hawk Press Poetry Book contest in 2020. Born in Brooklyn New York, a graduate of Haverford College, he began writing poetry after retiring from a thirty-five-year career in finance. He lives in Oakland, California with his wife, Liz.

Isa Maloof is a recipient of the Iris Starn Fellowship and the Saint Mary's Teaching Fellowship, where she recently graduated with an MFA in Poetry. A practitioner of Shambhala Buddhism for many years, she studied religions and translation at Harvard University and UC Berkeley. Isa is mama to three astonishing children and is the regional chair for Kundiman Northern California.

Genay Markham, Iris Starn Fellow, is a skilled writer and passionate leader with over 20 years of experience in youth development, leadership development, and social justice. She holds a Master of Fine Arts in Writing with a concentration in Creative Nonfiction from Saint Mary's College of California and a Bachelor of Science degree in Community and Regional Development from the University of California, Davis. Through her work as a writing tutor, leadership coach, and mentor, she uses storytelling to explore identity, resilience, and transformation while empowering others to find and use their voice.

Erica Matias is a high school student from Oakland who enjoys trying new things. Her poetry is inspired by the people who matter most in her life.

Fiona McFarlane's book of short stories *Highway Thirteen* won The Story Prize for 2024. "Demolition" appears in that book. Her first novel, *The Night Guest*, won several prizes including the Voss Literary

Prize and a New South Wales Premier's Award. It was also shortlisted for the *Guardian* First Book Award, Miles Franklin Literary Award, and *Los Angeles Times* Book Prize for First Fiction, among others. She is also the author of a short-story collection, *The High Places*, which won the International Dylan Thomas Prize. Her stories have appeared in *The New Yorker*, *Zoetrope: All-Story*, and *Best Australian Stories*. Her second novel, *The Sun Walks Down*, was published in Australia (October 2022), the United States (February 2023), and the UK (March 2023). McFarlane grew up in Sydney, Australia and now lives in the San Francisco Bay Area, where she teaches at the University of California, Berkeley.

Alexis Montifar is a sophomore at Northgate High School. She has an affinity for perplexing fictional literature. This is her first publication.

JR Murray was a professor of writing at the University of Southern California for over two decades, where he emphasized collaborations between his students and partners from the surrounding community. His work has appeared in *Gold Man Review, The Los Angeles Times, Avalon Literary Review, Big Muddy, Delmarva Review, and El Portal.* He serves on the NewLit Board of Directors.

Joyce Carol Oates is Joyce Carol Oates. She is a recipient of the National Humanities Medal, the National Book Critics Circle Ivan Sandrof Life Achievement Award, the National Book Award, the Jerusalem Prize for Lifetime Achievement, the Prix Femina, and the Cino Del Duca World Prize. She has been nominated several times for the Pulitzer Prize. She has written some of the most enduring fiction of our time, including the national best sellers *We Were the Mulvaneys, Blonde,* and the *New York Times* best seller *The Falls*. She is the Roger S. Berlind '52 Distinguished Professor of the Humanities Emerita at Princeton University and has been a member of The American Academy of Arts and Letters since 1978. Her Substack is "A Writer's Journal," and her most recent books include *Butcher*, *Babysitter*, and *Fox*. She is an honorary director of New Literary Project.

H. L. Onstad's writing has appeared in *ZYZZYVA*, *Harvard Review*, *Kirkus Reviews*, *Solstice Literary Magazine*, *Simpsonistas, Vol. 6*, and *HA Journal*, a publication of the Hannah Arendt Center for Politics and Humanities.

Lori Ostlund is the author of *Are You Happy?* (Astra House, May 2025). Her novel *After the Parade* (Scribner, 2015) was a B&N Discover pick, a finalist for the Center for Fiction First Novel Prize, and a NYTimes Editors' Choice. Her first book, *The Bigness of the World* (UGA, 2009; Scribner, 2016), received the Flannery O'Connor Award for Short Fiction, the Edmund White Debut Fiction Award, and the California Book Award for First Fiction. Her stories have appeared in the *Best American Short Stories*, the *PEN/O. Henry Prize Stories*, *ZYZZYVA*, and *New England Review*, among other places. Lori has received a Rona Jaffe Foundation Award and was a finalist for the Joyce Carol Oates Prize. She has served as the series editor of the Flannery O'Connor Award since 2022 and is on the board of the Barbara Deming Memorial Fund. She lives in San Francisco with her wife, the writer Anne Raeff. www.loriostlund.com

Anali Pascual is a junior at Oakland Charter High School. She wrote this poem to someone she likes, which got messy after she gave him two pieces of homemade chocolate.

Michael Ross is an Emeritus Director of New Literary Project. He earned his BA with distinction (1970) and his JD (1977) from the University of Virginia. He ended his career in the Navy as a Lieutenant and Operations Officer of the USS Truckee. He was a corporate lawyer, specializing in mergers and acquisitions, at Latham & Watkins and later served as Senior Vice President and General Counsel at Safeway Inc. He was a visiting lecturer at the University of Virginia and Berkeley Schools of Law, Peking University's School of Transnational Law, Dubrovnik International University, and the IE Law School in Madrid. He and his wife, Virginia, live in Orinda, California, and have a son, Charlie (30), and a daughter, Margaret (28). He is the author of Ross's Discoveries, nine books of quotations on a wide variety of topics collected from his reading of literary fiction since 1970.

Zara Sharza is a junior at Northgate High School. This is the first time Zara's work has been published, and she is so happy to see it in print!

Heather Tone is a recipient of the APR/Honickman First Book Prize for her poetry collection *Likenesses* (Copper Canyon Press) and the author of a poetry chapbook, *Gestures* (The Catenary Press). Her poems have appeared in *The Boston Review, The Colorado Review, Fence*, and other journals. In 2024, she received a Jack Hazard Fellowship from the New Literary Project for her fiction. A graduate of the Iowa Writers' Workshop, she currently lives and teaches in Austin.

Born and raised in Reno, Nevada, **Willy Vlautin** is a 2025 Recipient of the Joyce Carol Oates Prize. He is the author of seven novels and is the founder of the bands Richmond Fontaine and The Delines. Vlautin started writing stories and songs at the age of eleven after receiving his first guitar. Inspired by songwriters and novelists like Paul Kelly, Willie Nelson, Tom Waits, William Kennedy, Lucia Berlin, and John Steinbeck, Vlautin works diligently to tell working class stories in his novels and songs. Vlautin has been the recipient of three Oregon Book Awards, The Nevada Silver Pen Award, and was inducted into the Nevada Writers Hall of Fame and the Oregon Music Hall of Fame. He was a finalist for the PEN/Faulkner Award and was shortlisted for the International Dublin Literary Award. Three of his novels, *The Motel Life, Lean on Pete,* and *The Night Always Comes* have been adapted as films. His novels have been translated into fourteen languages. Vlautin teaches at Pacific University's MFA in Writing program and lives near Portland, Oregon with his wife, dog, cats, and horses.

Kalaijah Walker (She/Her) is a sixteen-year-old high school student. She was born and raised in Oakland. She loves horror movies and fantasy books. She is much more of an observer than a writer, but that doesn't stop her from trying her best.

David Wood has recently retired after teaching English at Northgate High School since 1984. He is a member of the New Literary Project Board; he also served on the jury for the Joyce Carol Oates Prize. He was a board member and board president of the celebrated Aurora Theatre Company, and now serves on the Advisory Board for the Kalmanovitz School of Education at Saint Mary's College of California. A Yale graduate and University of Chicago M.A., he estimates he taught for around one hundred years. In the words of his cherished author, Kurt Vonnegut, "So it goes."

Yarelie is a junior at Albany High. Her favorite thing to do is create art and after graduating she plans to go to a university and apply for a Disney internship. Her dream is to one day be able to have a job where she can enjoy creating her own work.

Rayjon Briscoe Young is a student, visual artist, civil servant, educator, and writer. Growing up in Oakland, California, and Brooklyn, New York, heavily informs his worldview when crafting stories. Rayjon's speculative writing typically aligns with horror, often framed within socio-political commentaries, magical realism, techno-realism, afrofuturism, fantasy, and bizarre science fiction.

Matthew Zapruder is the author of six collections of poetry, most recently *I Love Hearing Your Dreams* (Scribner, 2024), as well as two books of prose: *Why Poetry* (Ecco, 2017) and *Story of a Poem* (Unnamed, 2023). He is editor at large at Wave Books, where he edits contemporary poetry, prose, and translations. From 2016-7 he held the annually rotating position of Editor of the Poetry Column for the New York Times Magazine, and was the Editor of *Best American Poetry 2022*. He teaches in the MFA in Creative Writing Program at Saint Mary's College of California.

NEW LITERARY PROJECT TENTH ANNIVERSARY

2015–2025

Since 2015 NewLit has been mixing it up. The choice is clear. Fund the arts. As much as you can. Educate kids, support artists. Yes, the planet needs rescuing, and people need food and housing and health care. The world needs all that and more. The world also needs the nourishment, refuge, and attention of the arts. Young people who are marginalized—now speaking in their own voices. Writers now telling, and teachers now teaching, the stories of our lives. That's what helps make democracy a *democracy*. That's what NewLit is doing. Thank you for choosing to join with us. (Not exactly an elevator pitch. Which is fine by us. Because sometimes it's healthier to take the stairs.)

To donate to our 501(c)3 nonprofit, please visit
https://www.newliteraryproject.org/

Or better yet—mail your donation:
New Literary Project
4100 Redwood Road, Suite 20A/424
Oakland, CA 94619
EIN: 84-3898853

Or contact Diane Del Signore, Executive Director
diane@newliteraryproject.org

Your generosity today makes a difference *today*.
Write and read your heart out.

UMINOUS
A NOVEL
SILVIA PARK

THE SLIP
LUCAS SCHAEFER
a novel

FLORIDA PALMS
JOE PAN

MIDNIGHT
CINEMA PALACE

ANTONIO MICHAEL DOWNING
LACK CHEROKEE

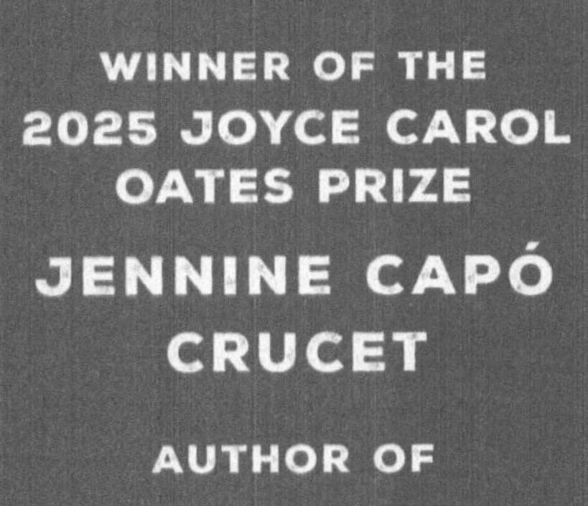
WINNER OF THE
2025 JOYCE CAROL
OATES PRIZE
JENNINE CAPÓ
CRUCET
AUTHOR OF
SAY HELLO TO MY
LITTLE FRIEND

Unforgettable Fiction from
SimonandSchuster.com

Portalmania
Stories
Debbie Urbanski

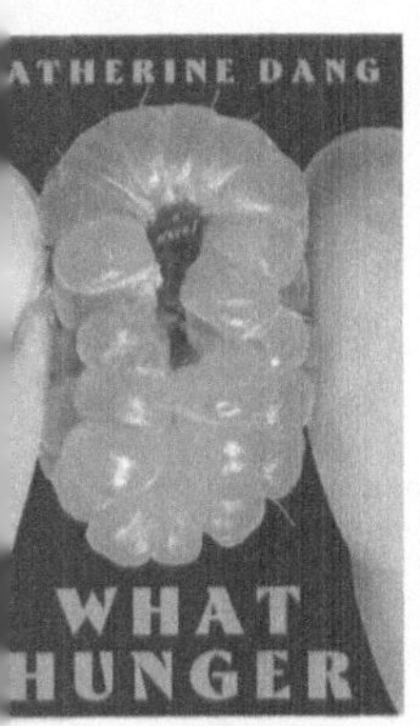
ATHERINE DANG
WHAT
HUNGER

NATIONAL BESTSELLER
HEARTWOOD
AMITY GAIGE

KERRY CULLEN
HOUSE
OF
BETH

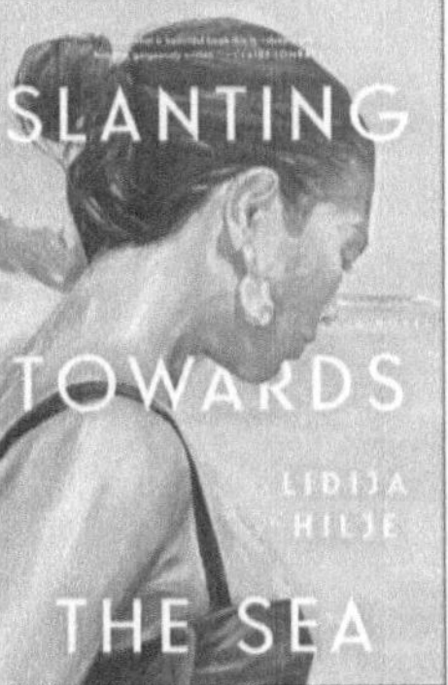
SLANTING
TOWARDS
THE SEA
LIDIJA
HILJE

AT
LAST
A Novel
MARISA
SILVER

CAPE FEVER
A NOVEL
NADIA DAVIDS

www.ingramcontent.com/pod-product-compliance
Lightning Source LLC
Chambersburg PA
CBHW050105170726
48245CB00001B/3
* 9 7 8 1 6 4 4 2 8 5 6 0 2 *